SPIRIT RELEASE

A PRACTICAL HANDBOOK

Sue Allen

Winchester, UK
Washington, USA)

First published by O Books, 2007
O Books is an imprint of John Hunt Publishing Ltd.,
The Bothy, Deershot Lodge,
Park Lane, Ropley, Hants, SO24 0BE, UK
office1@o-books.net
www.o-books.net

Distribution in:

UK and Europe
Orca Book Services
orders@orcabookservices.co.uk
Tel: 01202 665432 Fax: 01202 666219 Int. code (44)

USA and Canada
NBN
custserv@nbnbooks.com
Tel: 1 800 462 6420 Fax: 1 800 338 4550

Australia and New Zealand
Brumby Books
sales@brumbybooks.com
Tel: 61 3 9761 5535 Fax: 61 3 9761 7095

Far East (offices in Singapore, Thailand, Hong Kong, Taiwan)
Pansing Distribution Pte Ltd
kemal@pansing.com
Tel: 65 6319 9939 Fax: 65 6462 5761

South Africa
Alternative Books
altbook@peterhyde.co.za
Tel: 021 447 5300 Fax: 021 447 1430

Text copyright Sue Allen 2007

Design: Stuart Davies

ISBN-13: 978 1 84694 033 0
ISBN-10: 1 84694 033 8

A CIP catalogue record for this book is available from the British Library.

Printed and bound by CPI Group (UK) Ltd, Croydon, CR0 4YY

SPIRIT RELEASE

A PRACTICAL HANDBOOK

Sue Allen

BOOKS

Winchester, UK
Washington, USA

Dedication

For my parents who have always unconditionally loved and supported me in whatever direction I have taken.

CONTENTS

ACKNOWLEDGMENTS

I have had the honor to work with many people from very varied walks of life who required spirit release. Some of their stories have been included and their names and other identifying details have been omitted or changed to protect their confidentiality. I thank all of my clients and also the numerous students with whom I have worked. Through their interest, questions and accounts of their own experiences, I too have learned a great deal.

I would like to thank my homeopath, Marie-Anne Passchier-Sassen, not only for my greatly improved health and well-being, but for pointing me in the direction of the College of Psychic Studies all those years ago. Without her guidance I may not have commenced my spiritual journey or be working with Spirit as I am today.

I also thank the College of Psychic Studies for the excellence of their training and for allowing me to pass on my knowledge to others.

I am eternally grateful to Angela Palmer for her excellent editorial skills, searching questions and sense of humor, but most of all for her support and friendship.

PREFACE

As a child I saw and heard spirits, particularly at night when I was supposed to be settling down to sleep. At that time in my life I was afraid of many of them as I was not aware of why they were there or what they wanted. Some were very distressed and I would hear terrible sobs of despair and feel helpless.

My initiation into the darker end of spirit release came at the age of twenty one while at college and it took three months to realize there was actually nothing for me to fear. During one term a friend and I had experienced rooms being trashed in seconds without a sound, objects disappearing and reappearing, bad smells, freezing temperatures on very hot sunny days, a creeping cold heavy pressure and paralysis at night in bed, and being shown and told horrible things by the spirit that had arrived attached to a book about Saint Augustine. A Catholic priest had been summoned and managed to stand in my room for all of five minutes before running out terrified never to return.

One day I was sitting trying to finish an essay before the deadline the next day. The spirit kept taking my coffee, cigarettes and matches and being generally disruptive while I worked. It then started to demand that I open the window. In anger I told the spirit that if it wanted the window open it should do so itself. There was silence. Suddenly I realized it couldn't open the window. The spirit needed me to unlock the handle and turn it. Without my behavioral, physical, emotional, verbal and mental responses the spirit had nothing. It needed me. In responding I was feeding it; I was giving the spirit energy. Once I had made that leap in understanding my fear and anger left me and I was back in control. Following that significant breakthrough I took power over the situation and was able to deal with it relatively easily and safely. The spirit was released and never returned to bother anyone again.

Since that time I have released many spirits, some human and others not. There is a very wide variety of spirits needing this work. Many are lost, confused and unaware that their physical bodies have died. There are numerous practitioners in the spirit release field who work with this end of the spectrum and rescuing these spirits is often a very loving and joyful experience. At the other extreme are the darker entities. Many practitioners choose not to work in this area as there is a higher level of difficulty and risk. Having had the experience I did with a very dark spirit at the age of twenty one enables me to work at all levels.

One of the main issues I have learned is that however dark or abusive the entity there is always the need for compassion as well as assertiveness and intelligent discussion. I do not approve of screaming, shouting at, or abusing any spirit. If I was an earthbound spirit I would not find it at all helpful. In fact, I would probably retreat into increasingly defensive and antagonistic behavior and language. As a spirit this would not assist in my understanding of the situation or allow me to develop trust in the therapist who was attempting to carry out the release. As a healer I always try to work with entities the way I would wish to be worked with if I were in their situation. This does not mean that I let them get away with anything unacceptable. It does mean that my aim is to re-educate and provide a different option to the one in which the spirits find themselves.

Having spent some years carrying out this work with people

and places plus teaching workshops and classes on the subject I decided it was time to write this book. I wanted to give the answers and explanations to many of the questions that I have been asked time and time again. I always say to students that they should accept whatever resonates with them. No one should view a teacher, an author or anyone else for that matter, as having all of the answers. We do not have to take one person's statements as gospel and live by that for the rest of our lives. All of us have access to the wisdom and teachings from Spirit. What we think at one time may not be what we believe years down the line. We always have the opportunity to re-think, re-evaluate and develop what we accept as true. In my view this is the healthy way to be. There are times when we are not yet ready for certain information and may dismiss it, only to return to it at a later date finding it to be exactly what we need. I therefore ask you to read this book with an open mind, taking on board whatever feels right for you. I am not asking you to believe or agree with everything I have written, but I do ask you to accept it as my experience.

I have developed the view over time that nothing is impossible. In spirit release the impossible happens and the "rules" are broken. I have had experiences and met entities, even extra-terrestrials, that at one time I would not have believed possible. This leads me onto the question of how we know if something is our imagination or real. Generally the rule is that if it is real then the image or thought tends to come very suddenly into your head or senses and remain as it appeared. Often what you receive is a great surprise and not at all what you were expecting. You cannot change or build upon the image or the words received. For example, when I first consciously worked with a Spirit Guide I suddenly saw a blue vase.

I was surprised to see it and not receiving any verbal explanation from the Guide as to what it meant I tried to change it. I found I was unable to send it away, change the color or the shape. I couldn't put a flower in it, turn it upside down or do anything else with the vase. My lesson with that particular Guide was how to work with images and symbols. I can now talk for about twenty minutes on the significance of the blue vase if it comes up in a psychic reading!

On the other hand you can change an image produced by your imagination. So if you imagine a tree you can play with that image. Perhaps you might change the color of the leaves or its environment; you might add a bird in the branches and a cat clawing at the trunk. So very simply, in spirit release you may see or hear the entity and its appearance or words might be surprising or even shocking. What is particularly significant is when the client also sees, hears or senses exactly the same images and information as you. At the end of the day it is all about experience, trusting and knowing when what you see and sense is real.

The other phenomena that has taken place many times over the years is that clients and students have regularly reported that I have appeared in their dreams if ever they are faced with a negative entity. Some have also remembered calling me in their frightening dreams or in some cases have actually told the entity that they are going to summon me at which point the entity apparently disappears very fast! I have been fully aware on some of these occasions of finding myself on the astral plane and of banishing an entity. On others I have no memory of the occurrence, which does not necessarily mean that it did not happen, just that my physical body and conscious mind do not remember the activities of my astral body that night. Many healers, spirit release therapists and teachers find themselves continuing to work after their physical body falls asleep. Perhaps you are one of them. If so remember to work on your grounding and protection, particularly before sleep.

Don't forget that you are never alone. I could not do this work if I did not have constant assistance from the Beings of Light that are accessible to us all. It is not me that does the work; I facilitate the process. I never forget this fact and am forever grateful for being given the opportunity to be of service.

Sue Allen, MA, B.Ed (Hons), Dip APH, MNFSH, HMCPS
www.sueallentherapies.co.uk

CHAPTER 1
WHAT IS SPIRIT RELEASE?

The existence of discarnate spirits has been acknowledged since human history began. Shamanism is man's oldest form of relationship to Spirit and is thought to date back to the Neolithic period. The Shaman is known to work with spirit helpers including those of animals, and to drive spirits out of people in order to cure physical and mental illness. This practice of releasing spirits from people and places has become commonly known as exorcism and is an ancient part of the belief system of many world religions.

Exorcism or the casting out of demons was carried out by Jesus in the Bible. In Kabbalah a malicious spirit called a "dybbuk" is exorcised in a prescribed religious rite. Islam recognizes the need for exorcism of the "Jinn" or "Djinn." The Catholic Church developed an ancient ritual to expel a spirit and this Rite of Exorcism was revised in January 2000 and includes a warning not to confuse mental illness with demonic possession. Pope John Paul II personally performed three exorcisms between 1982 and 2001 during his tenure as pope.[1] The author and psychiatrist M. Scott Peck has performed two exorcisms[2] and the actor, writer and director Richard Rossi has filmed exorcisms in his documentary *Quest for Truth* in 1992.

In 2006 the BBC broadcast a documentary called *Witch Child*[3] which highlighted the plight of young children in the Congo who are being ejected from their homes or even killed because they have "kindoki" or spirit possession. These children are often placed on a fast with no food or water for many days, they are beaten, tortured, held over fire and chili peppers rubbed in their eyes. The program disclosed how supposedly "Christian" churches in the Congo and the UK are using aggressive deliverance techniques in an attempt to cure these children.

Exorcism or, what I and many others prefer to call it, spirit release or rescue, is carried out today by many people across the world in a gentle and compassionate way. Despite its long history the practice of spirit release or exorcism has frequently been kept hidden. Even today it is something that is often viewed as strange or frightening and many people deny that spirit attachment is a real phenomenon or believe that it exists only in the mind and is borne from fear. However much some people would like the whole subject just to go away, the area of spirit release is real and becoming more widely recognized especially with the increasing coverage through the media and the courage of people who tell of their experiences. This book is an attempt to normalize what seems a scary subject, to open people's minds and to enable those who need help to access it.

Spirit release is a very wide and fascinating area which encompasses a number of topics including psychic attack, curses, witchcraft, spirit attachment, possession, soul retrieval, haunting, soul rescue, deliverance and exorcism to name but a few. I separate them for ease of understanding into the following:

- **Psychic Attack** involves an external energy which negatively impacts on our sense of wellbeing. It can therefore come from environmental factors as well as from living people.
- **Spirit Attachment** is the presence of a living or deceased

entity in the aura or energy field of a person and sometimes an object.

- **Possession** is where an entity has entered the person's body and is lodged within.
- **Haunting** is the term most often applied to buildings, sites or objects and involves for example, ghosts, poltergeists and imprints.

The term s**pirit release** is frequently used by healers and psychics to define the work they do in releasing and rescuing entities found with people, on land, in buildings and objects which are then redirected to somewhere more appropriate. This process should be carried out in a compassionate way and without blame or judgment of the spirit or of the individual who is seeking help.

Soul retrieval signifies the bringing back of a fragment of the Self that has left at a time of trauma and although still attached energetically to the person is disconnected from the consciousness. Fragments need to be re-integrated and not removed, so exact identification of the issue is essential.

Soul rescue is a term that can mean either spirit release or soul retrieval. Some therapists differentiate between **release** as meaning the removal of an invading spirit while **rescue** indicates the removal of a trapped spirit. The difference being one of intention on the part of the entity.

The word **exorcism** is utilized today mainly by the Catholic Church. Many churches of other denominations prefer to use the term **deliverance.** Deliverance involves the recital of prayers with the person affected. Exorcism is carried out by a specially trained Catholic priest who performs the prescribed Rite of Exorcism which includes formal prayers and rituals designed to forcibly expel the spirit which is invariably viewed as evil. When asked if I do exorcisms I therefore say "no" as I do not hold the view that all entities are malevolent nor that people with attachments are at fault and should be made to feel guilty. It is true that spirits attach to us if we have an energy they need, for example an angry spirit may attach to an angry person. However, I have also come across cases where the person has simply been in the wrong place at the wrong time or there has been a karmic issue to be resolved through the experience of having a spirit attachment.

The word **entity** is defined in the Oxford Dictionary[4] as "a thing with distinct existence" and can therefore be applied to incarnate/living people as well as discarnate/deceased people, spirits, ghosts, demons, thought forms, extraterrestrials, animals, elementals, Guides and Angels.

Having established the basic definitions and concepts which will be examined in depth later in this book there is a need to recognize that spirit release, the term I shall use throughout, covers a very diverse spectrum of work. At one end there are the lost human souls who became confused after their death and at that moment didn't know where to go or what to do, or those who wanted to stay with a loved one or had unresolved issues. As a psychotherapist I often find myself in a counseling session with a spirit in preparation for their letting go, just as the living host often requires preparation before allowing the spirit to depart. This end of the spirit release spectrum can be very joyful and loving. Many healers, psychics and other practitioners are happy to release these spirits into the Light and it is often very easy and quick to do so.

At the other end of the spectrum are the demonics, the Dark

Force Entities, commonly referred to as DFEs. These are often not easy to release and should not be worked with unless you are competent to do so. Sometimes people come to me who have removed an entity from another person and allowed it to attach to themselves instead and then cannot dislodge it. If you want to work with the darker energies, training and experience as well as a thorough understanding of yourself are imperative. It is essential that you are able to work free from fear. Many people who work with this extreme end of spirit release have undergone an initiation to push their boundaries and find their limitations. This is because many of the demonic entities will try to discover your weak point. They will find your fear, anger, guilt or poor self esteem and will use these weaknesses to destroy you if they can. There is the possibility of serious danger to your mental, physical, emotional and spiritual wellbeing. In some cases people have died, often through suicide, due to spirit attachment or possession.

It is not an area that should be dabbled with for the sake of trying to help someone else and very likely making things worse for both of you. It is also not a subject to become so focused upon that every client is diagnosed as having at least one entity. It is vital that if there is no external force affecting the person coming to you for assistance that you tell them so. This enables them, if they choose, to start dealing with their own issues rather than projecting onto some other cause such as a spirit attachment or a psychic attack. I do not consider it helpful to collude with people who are in denial of a personal problem and seeking to blame someone or something else. There is also a need for clear discernment to ensure that the "entity" is not your own projection or creation. It is certainly not an area to become involved with through a need for glamour and ego building.

Throughout the book I give suggestions and techniques that may be helpful to the reader. However, in the more complex or dangerous areas I do not detail the methods used as they require professional intervention. Some of the work in clearing spirits and psychic attack is highly specialized and requires extensive training and self-development. The primary rule of first aid is to keep yourself safe before going to the assistance of another person. It is exactly the same in spirit release work. If you are not safe, sufficiently protected or experienced you may find yourself in significant danger.

I always tell people that I never work alone because I have a team of Light Beings, Guides, Angels, Ascended Masters and various helpers who work with me and provide guidance and protection. There are many techniques that can be used in this work which are very effective. Some spirit release therapists develop and perfect one specific procedure. Others use a variety of practices according to need. It is important to respect the various techniques, but also to recognize that people and spirits are individual so what works for one may not work for another and each scenario may be quite different.

It is essential that spirit release is carried out responsibly. I always ask that the spirit is taken to a place that is appropriate and from where it cannot return. It is not sufficient to diagnose a spirit presence and banish it through an open window or door as you are merely passing the problem onto an unsuspecting passer-by.

There are some individuals with entities who do not see a major improvement in their situation after initial treatment and go from therapist to therapist in their search for relief. There are many reasons for this. It may be that the therapist is not energetically able to remove that particular type of entity. It can be that the client is not yet ready or able to let the entity go. In many situations of problematic spirit release the client is allowing the situation and it may take time to find out why. Perhaps the method being used is not the right one, for example some people respond well to hypnotherapy and others do not. If there is a karmic issue involved perhaps it has not yet been fully understood and therefore remains unresolved. In some cases there are layers of entities with one person and it is a bit like peeling an onion, sometimes with the most problematic entity in the last layers. I have met a few people who have continued to deliberately collect entities because otherwise they would be lonely, isolated and consider themselves to be without a role or function. It may also be that no entity is present and the person needs to look at their psychological, emotional or lifestyle issues.

Sometimes the client wants to believe they have an entity with them when in fact they do not. I met one man who had a spirit attachment called "Henry" removed by another therapist, but had then recreated the spirit in a thought form so he could continue to travel around the country working with therapists to remove "Henry." Others insist they are possessed when they actually have a mental health problem, as has happened in a number of cases with which I have worked. These clients are often unhappy with my view of what is happening. Some of these people, as far as I know, are still trying to find someone to remove their "spirits." Latest statistics show that one in four adults in the UK[5] and also in the USA[6] experience a mental health problem at any one time. This can include anything from panic attacks, anxiety, depression and phobias to schizophrenia or bipolar disorder. The symptoms of a mental illness can be very similar to those of spirit attachment. It would be interesting to investigate how many people have been misdiagnosed.

It is important to note at this point that spirit attachment or possession is a common cause of mental health problems and also of drug and alcohol use. These scenarios often indicate a "chicken and egg" situation in that the individual may have developed a drug/alcohol problem which has attracted a spirit or conversely, the invasion by a spirit has caused the problematic drug/alcohol use. In the latter case the problem often starts quite suddenly and the release of the earthbound spirits leads to a cessation or at least a reduction of the drug/alcohol use. The individual may still have to work on the physiological and psychological effects of their drug/alcohol use and unlearn their behavior and recognize the triggers for their addiction. In the first case scenario where the individual's drug/alcohol use has attracted the spirit the person still has to deal with their own addictive behavior, although they may now be more motivated to do so having experienced the effects of having a   discarnate spirit or two with them.

The mental health scenario is similar to the drug/alcohol one above, in that sometimes the spirit attachment has caused a psychotic episode leading to medical treatment. In other cases admission to a mental health hospital means the person is in an undeniably vulnerable state and more open to spirit attachment. It is well known that places such as hospitals, pubs, clubs and graveyards are likely places to pick up unseen spirits. It is often the case that the medication given to stop the voices or to sedate unwanted behavior has little or no effect. The medication dosage may be increased in order to affect any change, but have various distressing side effects. Sometimes a heavy dosage will stop the voices and interference, but when the medication is reduced the voices return indicating that they have not disappeared and their volume has just been turned down for a while. A spirit release however, if that is the underlying problem, can have an immediate effect. In other cases the attached spirit has caused physiological and psychological problems especially if it has been there for a while. This means that any improvement may be more gradual or that the person afflicted may still experience some mental health issues, albeit lessened. I have found it is important in most cases of spirit attachment to release the spirit as quickly as possible after connection. Firstly because it is easier to do so and secondly because the entity has the opportunity to do far less damage. I have worked with many people who have carried their spirits around with them for anything up to fifty years, sometimes unknowingly and sometimes because they have simply not been aware that help was available.

Spirit attachment or psychic attack can happen to virtually anyone of any class, race or culture. I have worked with all types of people both adults and children, of all religious and spiritual beliefs, living very different lives. I have cleared drug users, sex workers, alcoholics, criminals and those who are mentally ill as well as doctors, psychiatrists, psychologists, nurses, social workers, journalists, actors, counselors, healers, spirit release therapists, office and bank workers, police and fire officers. There should be no shame or guilt attached to the fact that you might have collected a spirit or two or have been subjected to a psychic attack. In all events it should be viewed as a learning experience.

In this book I aim to give as much information as possible on the types of entities that exist, how and why they arrive, the signs and symptoms of their presence and the various treatment options. In teaching this subject I always aim to give students enough information to enable recognition of the problem, decide if they are competent to deal with it or whether the case needs referral to someone who is.

I ask that the reader treat the information in this book wisely and use it proficiently and therefore safely if called upon to do so. Ensure you have the skills and insurance required before carrying out a spirit release and if in doubt, *don't!*

CHAPTER TWO
PSYCHIC ATTACK

What Is Psychic Attack?

Psychic attack is a very widely used term which is often misunderstood. It means that an external energy affects you in such a way that it has a detrimental effect on your sense of well-being. Our well-being includes our physical, emotional, mental and spiritual functioning and generally denotes a sense of harmony and balance in our lives. It is possible to see from this wide definition that psychic attack can therefore include environmental energy which causes us discomfort such as bright lights, noise and pollution. The other types of psychic attack come from living people and include psychic vampirism, witchcraft, curses, black magic, cords and thought forms which will all be covered in detail. In all cases of psychic attack we need to look at the reason for the attack and take responsibility for why we have allowed it to affect us. It is essential to recognize that ultimately someone can only attack you if allowed to. This applies to all forms of psychic attack including both the intentional and the unintentional. I personally do not include spirit attachment or possession in this area for the sake of simplicity, although the presence of entities can clearly affect our sense of well-being.

The subject of psychic attack necessarily includes a discussion of intention as some attacks are deliberate, but many are not. As we go about our daily lives we find ourselves in situations with the opportunity for our energy to be affected in a negative way.

For example, you get on a train or bus and sit down on an empty seat. The energy of the last person who sat there may still be present and you could be affected by it. If that person had a wonderful, gentle, warm, loving energy then that journey could be a very enjoyable one. If however, the person was feeling upset or angry then you may well feel very uncomfortable, perhaps without knowing why. This can be extended into sleeping in hotel beds, borrowing someone else's coat or even lying on a massage or healing couch that has not been energetically cleared between clients.

You may also find that you suddenly develop a headache or other symptom when in a crowd. Consideration always needs to be given as to whether this headache is actually yours. One very easy way to establish this is by asking yourself "is this headache mine?" You will find that you receive an answer even if you have not done this before. The answer can simply be a physical reaction of the body or a knowing or you may even hear a "yes" or "no" in your mind. If you realize that the headache is not yours then you can ask that it is removed, perhaps thinking "I release this headache into the Universe." The headache will magically disappear and the negative energy will be safely transmuted. You do not need to try to establish whose headache it was and under no circumstances should you send it back to them. If the headache is yours then you should take an aspirin or do whatever you normally do for a headache.

We now see that these forms of psychic attack are not intended by the people involved. It is also not for us to act as judge and jury and send negative energy back to people except in exceptional circumstances. The usual maxim is one of "stop not harm." The

Law of the Universe dictates that whatever we give out will always come back to us, whether immediately or very much later. In some instances it may come back in a different lifetime when we perhaps experience a similar situation again, but from another point of view or position. In my mind karma is about a need to experience, learn and understand. It is not about punishment. I do not believe for example, that people who are born into this life with a serious disability or disadvantage are being punished for something they did in a previous life. I find it an interesting view to consider that people with severe learning difficulties may be advanced souls who are here to teach love. People with Downs Syndrome for example, are generally very affectionate and loving and teach this to others.

In each lifetime I believe that we exist to have both positive and negative experiences in order to learn from them. I also believe that we choose those lessons before we are born. If we do not learn what we were supposed to from one experience the Universe provides the lesson for us again. Some people therefore recognize patterns in their lives which may be repeated many times until the understanding takes place. If we accept this view then people affected by spirit attachment and psychic attack have actually chosen that experience in their current lifetime. A number of people who experience these types of problems go onto help others through healing or psychic work or by being able to recognize the problem and refer to an appropriate practitioner.

What we do have to be clear about is that it is our responsibility to be aware of our own energy and to protect it from negativity. It is also essential that we are responsible for our thoughts and actions. You may have heard the expression "energy follows thought." We are all energetic beings and therefore connected to everything around us. Everything that we think, feel and do has an impact and this can be on a micro or a macro level. Our thoughts leave our energy field like radio waves and therefore have the power to affect others especially if they are intensified by strong emotions. For example, you leave a meeting at work feeling particularly angry with someone who attended. For the next twenty minutes you think or even verbally express those angry thoughts about that person, perhaps fantasizing about what you would like to do to them or what you should have said. The person that you are so angry with may well feel your angry thoughts in the form of physical pain or nausea. You have, albeit unaware, just carried out a psychic attack.

We are all human and may feel angry, upset or jealous at times. When you are aware however, of the potential impact of your feelings or thoughts on others you can then do something about it. Just as you did with the headache described earlier you can ask the Universe, the Earth, your God, your Guide or Angel to remove the negative energy you have sent to the other person. You may also like to imagine that person surrounded in Light and ask that they receive healing. I suggest that you also give yourself some healing at the same time. The power of the mind and your intention is enormous. If you use your intention effectively and without allowing doubt to creep in then it is very strong. For example, to say "I am protected" and to know it absolutely means that you are. I often use my intention when I sit next to someone or work with a client who has a cold or flu by saying mentally "I am not going to catch that cold/flu" and more often than not I remain well.

Psychic Vampires

Psychic vampires can work intentionally or completely unconsciously. Instead of sucking blood as in the movies they suck
our life force or energy. We have all met people or have friends or
even partners and parents who act in this way. For example, you
have a friend who you meet for coffee or who phones you to
offload their latest problems. After half an hour they feel great and
you feel completely drained. What has taken place is the process of
osmosis where they have absorbed your energy. Energy like water
will find a balance and flow to the lowest point if allowed to. So if
your energy is high and your friend's energy is low they may
connect to you and draw on your energy to increase their own. You
may feel this effect if you visit an ill, weak or older person where
their need for strength and perhaps even survival causes them to
unconsciously feed on your energy. Other vampires are very
demanding of your time and attention and are possibly more aware
of what they are doing. I have known people who have visited a
healer or a masseur where afterwards they always felt completely
drained and even unwell. My advice is to change their therapist.

If you are a practitioner or therapist, certain of your clients may
also want energy from you. As healers we channel energy through
ourselves for others – this is not the same as allowing people to
take or even giving them our own energy. Maybe you are a
naturally giving person or even a rescuer who allows others to
absorb your energy. It is important to recognize who has this
draining effect on you and to take responsibility for not allowing it
to continue. Over time people who allow the psychic vampire to
continue sucking their energy will probably become unwell and
exhausted. At that point the vampire will invariably move onto

someone else who can provide a good source of what they need.

This leads us onto the intentional vampires who not only connect to others energetically in order to drain energy, but may also link in other ways. For example, many people wear jewelry such as rings and bracelets. Have you ever had the experience of someone taking and keeping hold of your hand uninvited, often looking into your eyes at the same time? I am not talking about a loved one here, but someone that perhaps you do not know well or where it may be inappropriate to the situation. If that person holding your hand wishes to attach to you, or even program you to allow them to take your energy, this is a good opportunity for them to do so. The same can be done with your belongings such as objects or clothing. Once the program to allow the vampire access to your energy is in place, you could even keep this program running yourself. You may find it hard to stop thinking about the vampire or that it is impossible to refuse them when they make demands upon you.

In extreme circumstances some people experience night visits from the vampire and get a sense while lying in bed of an energy creeping up over them and a feeling of weight on the chest. These people often feel as if they cannot move or cry out and some victims have recognized the identity of the vampire. The person generally recovers while sleeping. There are of course, other reasons for this phenomenon which will be explored later when looking at entities. There are many myths and legends about vampires as explored by Konstantinos in his interesting book, *Vampires: The Occult Truth.*[7] I have worked with some cases of modern vampiric attack as described above. I have also worked with people who are unaware that they take other people's energy until it is pointed out to them and they are taught how to energize themselves more appropriately.

Psychic vampirism is implicated in the issue of cords which will be covered in the next chapter and also with witchcraft and black magic which will be discussed later. If faced with a situation of psychic vampirism you must learn how to protect against it while still being able to visit your elderly parent, see a friend for coffee and generally go about your daily life. Often a vampire will attach to your Solar Plexus chakra in order to gain control over you as well as drain your energy. A visualized shield, door or some other protective symbol used with intent across your abdomen from the diaphragm down to your pelvis should help. If you need fast protection, for example if you pick up the telephone and find the vampiric person on the other end, simply place a hand across your Solar Plexus in order to protect it. Attachments may also be made to other chakras including the Base/Root chakra, which governs your physical health and immune system, and also to organs and other parts of the body. This will be explored in depth in chapter 3.

At night it is always a good idea to protect yourself before going to sleep. It is also sensible to ensure you remain very grounded at all times as this keeps your energy safe. Grounding and protection will be dealt with in detail in chapter 10.

Cleansing is another essential area and it is important to keep your energy, chakras and aura as clear as possible to prevent negativity from sticking to the blocked or darker areas of your energy. If you feel your jewelry, personal objects or clothing have been contaminated then they need to be cleansed with the intention of disconnecting the vampire or any other form of psychic attack.

Methods of cleansing will also be covered in chapter 10.

If you wish to stop a vampire all of the above methods should be taken into consideration. The vampire's energy should be disconnected from yours and methods to do this are described in chapter 3 on cords. The key to the whole area of spirit release is protection and having an absolute belief that you are protected, otherwise whatever technique you use will not work effectively. As soon as doubt, fear and anxiety creep in then the attacker has the upper hand as you have given away your power.

It is essential to look at why you are allowing the vampire to take your energy. Sometimes it is a case of recognizing why you are both interacting in this way and taking the firm decision that you are not going to allow it to continue. You can tell your attacker this in meditation if you know their identity, by visualizing them in a bubble of Light, telling them that it is going to stop from that moment and sending them away in their bubble. Sometimes you find you are continually trying to stop the person attacking you and stealing your energy without success. It may be appropriate in some circumstances for you to physically talk to the vampire and point out what they are doing as it is possible that they are unaware of their attack. In others it may be necessary to cease all contact with them. If you are unable to stop the attacks yourself then seek help from a person experienced in this area.

CHAPTER THREE
CORDS

Cords are invisible energetic links between you and another person or object. The person with whom you are corded may be living or deceased. Many attached spirits use a cord to attach to their host and in releasing the spirit the cord has to be cut. You may also be corded to objects or living things that are important to you such as an animal, a house, an item of jewelry or ornament. You might be corded to something more abstract such as a goal or something that you wish to achieve in life. You may also cord to a thought form which will not be covered here, but in chapter 4. We naturally cord to other people and allow them to cord to us during our everyday lives. Many of these cords are short term and normally dissolve very quickly. It is generally the longer term cords that can cause problems for the people at the end of each cord. Some of these cords are made intentionally and others are formed unconsciously. They may be psychically seen or sensed within the aura, the chakras or attached to parts of the physical body.

Positive Cords

Cords between parents and their young children are both positive and necessary as they are a direct line of communication. Babies are naturally very dependant and vulnerable and part of the parental bonding is carried out by cording to at least one, but often all seven chakras. In this way parents are very aware of their child's needs and will often wake the instant their baby needs attention during the night. This type of cording allows the intuitive knowing of parents who feel a response if their child is in any form of distress or trouble. As the child grows and becomes more independent these cords should gradually start to disappear and this is thought to occur from the age of about seven years. Sometimes however, these cords are not dissolved naturally. This leads to adults remaining corded to one or both parents, often at the Solar Plexus which is the center for control. There may be cords to other chakras, for instance the Sacral or Base chakra, particularly if there has been parental sexual abuse of the child.

Heart chakra cords are very common in loving relationships and can be seen or sensed between parents and their children of any age, partners, family members and good friends. Between lovers it is common to see Heart and Sacral chakra cords indicating their loving and sexually intimate relationship. With positive cords visualization work can be carried out to strengthen, energize and refresh the cords perhaps strengthening a Heart cord by sending more love through the cord to your partner. A word of caution here. Do not try to form or strengthen a Heart cord to someone in order to make them love you. This amounts to manipulation of another person and is therefore an intentional form of psychic attack. Even if you succeeded in compelling that person to stay at your side, could you really be sure that they loved you? My view is that we can only ever change ourselves. We do not have the right to try to control or maneuver another person.

Another positive cord is the one between the physical and astral bodies usually thought to be connected at the Solar Plexus chakra. If you astral travel during sleep at night or consciously during the day your astral essence separates from the physical body, but remains attached on a very thin cord. This allows the astral part to travel and return safely without detrimental effect to the body. People often do this unknowingly during sleep and may remember a very vivid dream in which loved ones who have passed into the spirit world are met with and other dimensions visited. Sometimes the sense is of floating, flying or falling as the astral body moves above the sleeping corporeal form. If the traveler is disturbed by a sound or touch then the astral body returns very quickly and you may jump awake. It is suggested that any mirrors should be facing away from the bed or covered at night to prevent shock to the astral body as it rises from the sleeping figure.

Some people carry out remote healing or spirit release work by astral travel or projection and learn to control this process consciously. Astral projection means to consciously extend the astral body and awareness to another person or place. Astral travel means separation of the astral and physical bodies as described above. It is important that this is only carried out with permission, as in some cases the healer's astral body may be seen or felt by the person or place visited. This can cause a shock to the client or their family if they are not expecting to see you! The healer carrying out the astral travel or projection is able to see and feel everything that happens and can walk into rooms and speak with any spirits that may be present. This method is quite different to remote healing, often referred to as absent or distant healing, which does not use astral projection. In this case the astral body stays with the healer who works using visualization, prayer and intention to carry out the work.

Many people go out of their body at times of trauma or shock as a way of numbing the physical or emotional pain, but they remain attached on their astral cord and are therefore still able to operate the body while not fully in it. During surgery under general anesthetic the astral body or the consciousness leaves. In this instance, once the anesthetic wears off the astral form returns. A similar cord exists if a fragment of the self has left. In situations of trauma or stress a part of you may separate from the whole and while still attached via a thin cord may travel out into your aura or beyond. This can happen at any time from within the womb onwards and might occur at a time of serious trauma such as attempted abortion, abuse or major accident, or may have been caused in childhood, for example by moving house and having to leave school friends. In some cases people have been able to retrieve their fragment by revisiting their old house or the site of their accident. Soul retrieval is the process whereby the fragment is rescued and re-integrated into the body. A key part of this work is to find out why the fragment left, what it now needs and how those needs can be met. Healing of the wound or psychological issue as well as the aura needs to take place.

One very interesting case with whom I worked was a man in his fifties who had never managed to find a job or leave his parent's home. As I looked at him psychically I saw nine fragments still within his energy field, but separated just as if the jigsaw pieces had not yet been fitted together. I also saw a crowd of people with him. He told me that he had been born a rhesus negative baby. The shock of a traumatic birth and several complete blood transfusions had caused the fragmentation and had also brought the energy of the various blood donors into his very sensitive and open energy field. He had never recovered. I carried out a spirit release of the donor energies followed by integration and healing of the fragmentation. Unfortunately I do not know the result of this work as I did not meet the man again. I have a policy of not chasing people to see how they progress, but always give them the chance to contact me after a session with any issues that might arise. This is the case with many healers who do not feel that they can call people back for a follow-up appointment, especially if the client has traveled a distance or there is a session fee to pay. Sometimes I hear from people, months or years after carrying out a piece of work with them, that they have been overjoyed with the results.

Finding Cords

Many people are very good at visualization and it is quite possible to see a cord attached to you or to someone else. Numerous people do this with their eyes closed and some with the eyes open. Others are better at sensing cords and may find them by running a hand close to the body and feeling a change in energy through the hands. You can do this for yourself or practice on another person. An alternative method is to sense your physical body and feel where there is a pulling, tension or a block which might indicate a cord. Dowsers could use a pendulum while others may hear or intuitively know the name of the person to whom they are corded or where the cord is attached.

Cords may be of any size, texture, length or number. They are frequently described as a fleshy umbilical cord, a cable, or tree roots, sometimes with hooks or tentacles on the ends that entwine around the body or organs. The cords may have a color and I have found that the dark, black or brown cords are often very old and may be inactive or even dead. All of this information provides access to the nature of this cord. Is it a thick, powerful, pulsating cord which is fully energized and has hooks going deep within you? If so, there are still issues to resolve here as this cord is very much alive and probably having quite an effect on you. Is it on the other hand a thin, brittle, dark cord devoid of energy? This would indicate an old, dead cord that is no longer active and can easily be destroyed.

With all cords it is important to look at the direction in which the energy of the cord is flowing. Does it flow from you to the other person? From them to you? Or equally in both directions? I had a client arrive for an appointment saying that she was about to leave her husband of twenty years plus three children, her house and business for a new lover who was also married and living with his wife. She asked me to see what the outcome would be if she did this. As I looked at her I realized there was a Heart cord in place and was guided to work with her on this. In a visualization she easily identified the Heart cord between them and was very happy as she saw it as large, pink, alive and energized. I then asked her to look at the directions in which the energy in the cord ran and she confirmed that it did indeed run from her to her lover. However, she discovered with some horror that there was no energy running from him towards her. I then asked her to have a mental conversation with her lover and she realized that he did not reciprocate her feelings and had no intention of leaving his wife. At this point she insisted we cut the cord and she returned home to her husband and children.

Negative Cords

Negative cords can be formed both with and without intention.

Cords are formed very easily through developing a mental or emotional focus on someone. This creates the energetic link or cord. Intentional cords are made with the purpose of achieving something specific. It may be about forming a certain type of relationship with someone or controlling what they think or believe and how they behave. The intentional corder may not actually see a cord as such, but they will be conscious of their desire to affect the other person in some way. Cords made consciously can be very persistent and difficult to break so strength of intention is an important element to be aware of. Some of these intentional cords are found at the back of the body as the person connecting to you does not wish to be found out. This way of cording demonstrates the manipulative, devious and controlling nature of their intent. Cords often cause physical symptoms and at the back of the body can cause pain in the spine and the muscles. Some people will intentionally cord to you via another person, a pet or an object. In this event you may think that the cord in place is coming from your friend whereas they are being used to hide the real intruder. Both you and your friend may be affected by tiredness or any of the other symptoms outlined later. As we have seen, psychic vampires also often use cords to attach to us in order to drain our energy and to control us in some way.

Another very common scenario is at the end of a relationship when you may leave a part of yourself corded to your ex-partner or they may still be energetically with you in your aura. I often see other people standing in an individual's energy field and when I describe them I'm frequently told that they were either someone the person left many years before or they are a parent. If you are an experienced clairvoyant it is fairly easy to tell if the person you are seeing in the aura is deceased as they will be three dimensional and feel energetically different to someone still living who will be seen as two dimensional. In the case of spirit attachment there will often be a cording which allows the spirit to attach and to feed off your energy. In some cases I have found cords to people from the client's past lives. Some of these have been positive cordings to other members of their soul group. Members of a soul group will often reincarnate together through several lifetimes in order to provide support, but also lessons in that lifetime. Other past life cords are no longer beneficial to the person and the issues held there need to be worked with, understood, resolved and then cut.

Symptoms of a negative cording can include a sensation of pulling or tension at the connection point. Physical pain and illness can ensue. You may also feel uncentered and ungrounded. A cord can force the energy channel that runs down the center of your body out of line or keep a chakra stuck in a wide open condition. Cords at the back of the Heart center can prevent your Guides from connecting with you whereas cords at the head can interfere with your ability to meditate, visualize, dream or even think clearly.

How And Why

Have you ever been for a psychic reading and thought that the psychic was not reading you, but someone else? Some untrained psychics work by cording to you in order to read your information. If you have someone else also corded to you the psychic may well pick up information about the attached friend, partner or family member rather than you. On the other hand clients or sitters may cord to the psychic during the reading in their desperation to receive guidance. This happened to me on one occasion when I recognized after the sitting had ended that I had an extremely bloated abdomen, but had not eaten anything. I realized that the sitter had corded to my Solar Plexus with the aim of "help me, advise me, tell me what to do." I cut the cord and my stomach immediately returned to normal. So when we work with people, particularly if you are in the caring professions, counseling, healing or therapeutic body work for example, it is essential to recognize that cording is a possibility and to protect ourselves. Ultimately someone can only cord or remain corded to you if you allow them to. This happens through agreement, collusion or a lack of protection and self-awareness.

We also cord naturally to those with whom we have casual, intimate or co-dependant relationships and this may be through desire, need or strong emotions such as love, anger and jealousy. For example, you may need someone's energy and strength or desire that they stay with you with the underlying pleas of "don't go, don't change your job or be successful" or of "love me, look after me." We have all heard people say such things as "he is part of me," "she is hooked into me," "she has her claws in him," "I am obsessed with her," "I can't live without him," "I owe him/he owes me," "she needs me/I need her." These often hidden agendas include a desire for control, power and attention, the fear of change, loneliness or independence. People sometimes fear their relationships may change and therefore hold onto and block themselves or the other person from moving forwards. In this situation one or both people in the relationship can become stuck in depression, negativity, resentment or anger. One person may be needy and demanding, wanting to be taken care of and this can develop into an obsessional and jealous relationship with the aim of excluding other people. In time the couple may find that they feel isolated, bored and trapped. Neither can leave because they fear the other or even themselves would not survive.

Some people cord to others feeling that they are helping them to exist. I once worked with a man whose elderly mother was very dependent upon him. She had corded to his Solar Plexus which is the center we attach to if we want to control someone. When she needed her son she had only to think of him, energetically tugging the cord, and he would feel a sudden need to call her or visit. His mother had become so delighted with her ability to do this that she would wake him in the night without the use of the telephone and he would get out of bed to go to her house. The man was becoming more depleted and felt his life was not his own. He was trapped in the guilt of not wanting his mother to be so demanding, but also feeling burdened with the sole responsibility as the only child. He would have never forgiven himself if something had happened to her. I explained that if we cut the cord neither would be harmed, his mother would still exist and he would feel much better, less drained, more in control of the situation and therefore able to respond to her more positively and calmly. It was unlikely that his mother realized that the phenomenon of an actual cord existed, but she was clearly desiring her son's attention and therefore focusing her thoughts and emotional needs in his direction. After much discussion we did carry out a de-cording, but unfortunately for both of them, after he left they re-corded to each other because he felt so guilty.

People cord to us for our strengths, but may also attach to our weaker areas in order to control or manipulate our thoughts or behavior. Through a cord we can transfer energy in both directions. We can drain another person's energy or block them in some way as well as sending both negative and positive emotions, thoughts and physical feelings. In this way a cord can ensure you are stuck in negative thoughts, with feelings of low self-worth, lacking in both confidence and a sense of individuality, without flexibility or ability to change, dependent upon another or even acting as a doormat for them. It is therefore important to investigate the agenda in place. What is it that this person is investing in you or needing from you? If you cord to another person what do you lose, gain or have to give up by keeping or cutting the cord? If you understand the reasons behind the cord then it is easier to cut it and remain free from re-cording again.

Karmic Cords

At this point we need to explore the existence of karmic cords. These are often formed before entry into this incarnation to other people and soul mates with whom we have unresolved issues. A soul mate is not necessarily the person with whom we fall madly in love and live happily ever after. Our soul mate can be someone with whom we spend a period of time in order to work out some very deep, difficult issues before going our separate ways. Sometimes these issues can be traced back through centuries and may have been repeated many times. I am finding that many people in this lifetime are now having to deal with all of their outstanding issues that they have collected over other lives.

Sometimes there is a karmic cord to a contract that has been made either with others or with yourself. For example, if in other lifetimes you have done something that caused great distress you may then vow never to repeat the same experience. I worked with a young woman who was unable to conceive a child. As I worked in her energy field I saw an image of her in medieval times giving birth in a castle tower. She and her husband were very much in love and this would be their first child. Unfortunately the baby boy was breach and she was unable to deliver him. Both mother and baby died leaving a devastated husband. As she left the body the mother was unable to accept her death and stayed earthbound for some time in considerable distress over the effect on her husband and the loss of her child. In this lifetime she had been unable to conceive with the issues still held in her aura of "I cannot give birth" and "I can't do that to my husband." This client fully resonated with what emerged and so we were able to work on healing that past life experience for the three people involved.

The important thing to note is that a karmic cord cannot be cut until the karmic lesson has been faced, experienced, learned, fully understood and integrated. Once the issue is resolved with the person or contact and is let go of, then the cord can be released. If you find that a cord you cut keeps reforming it may well be a karmic cord that you have not yet fully understood.

Chakra Cords

Many cords are attached to one or more of the seven major chakras in the body and sometimes some of the minor ones such as at the palms of the hands and the soles of the feet. Cords may also be attached to body organs for example, the liver or spleen, both of which have major functions in terms of the blood, indicating a desire to drain this life force and often affecting the efficiency of these organs. I have also found people with cords binding their wrists, ankles, shoulders, waists, necks and so on. A number of people with whom I have worked have discovered a myriad of cords running to every area of the body or energy system. With these multiple cords they are not usually cut separately, but together as a whole.

So let us look at each of the major chakras and discover the reasons behind these cordings and the symptoms that may be experienced. It is important as you read the following that you do not become paranoid or over-identify with the symptoms outlined as they may be caused by something other than a cord. It is also imperative if you do have an energetic cord attached somewhere in your body that you recognize it is unlikely to cause all of the various illnesses listed. The symptoms you will possibly experience are often minor. The most serious effects are usually only feasible if the cord is particularly negative, destructive, intentional and long term. As in all cases where physical symptoms are experienced a doctor should be consulted to establish if there is a physiological cause.

When describing the chakra colors I have used the generally accepted Western system which uses the seven colors of the rainbow. These colors of red, orange, yellow, green, blue, indigo and violet have different vibrations, with red at the Base chakra as the slowest and violet at the Crown as the highest and finest energy. The rainbow signifies the link between Heaven and Earth and denotes magic and hope. Other systems use different colors for the chakras, for example gold or white for the Crown and pink for the Heart.

Base/Root Chakra

This chakra is found at the bottom of the spine at the perineum and is red in color. Babies need to be corded from here to their mother in order to keep them safe. This chakra is concerned with basic physical health and survival, grounding, stability and security. A child or adult who does not feel secure and grounded may well be physically small and underweight. If someone cords to you here they are probably attempting to make you feel insecure and vulnerable or even to affect your health or continued existence. The converse is that they want you to support them or diversely to have a sexual relationship with them.

With a cord at the Base/Root chakra your physical and sexual energy may be very depleted. You might also find it very difficult if not impossible to ground yourself and therefore may be quite clumsy, feel disorientated and disconnected. A lack of grounding in turn causes a weakened energy field and body. The victim may feel as if they are being punished without understanding the reason why. They may feel very isolated and lack a sense of who they are. The person can become very fearful and in severe cases become so depressed and anxious that they lose the will to live. Other people with a cord at this chakra may react with anger and aggression which after all are the opposites of fear.

Another effect of a cord at the Base chakra is depletion of the immune system leaving you more open to infections such as coughs and colds or more seriously can lead to immune system diseases or conditions. It may also affect the skeletal system, the adrenals causing restlessness, induce poor circulation which may mean you feel cold, affect digestion leading to constipation, cause hemorrhoids and in extreme cases may cause bowel cancer.

Sacral Chakra

This chakra is located just under the tummy button inside the lower abdomen and is orange. This is the center for sexuality and desire, identity and individuality, creative energy, emotions, appetite, money, and career. If someone cords to you here they are either asking for sex, passion, energy and motivation or trying to make you feel guilty and ashamed or wanting you to be less successful and enthusiastic.

With a cord connected to the Sacral center you may be emotionally unstable and insecure, prone to tears, possibly experience feelings of jealousy, rage, guilt and shame or conversely feel emotionally numb. You could experience a lack of self control, addictive behavior and eating disorders such as obesity or anorexia. There might be a sense of confusion with a lack of motivation, enthusiasm and ability to experience pleasure. A cord here can lead to problems with confidence, self identity and personal boundaries and a lack of success in work and financial affairs. People such as artists, writers and musicians may find that their creative energy decreases or becomes completely blocked.

Physically a cord at the Sacral chakra can produce stomach bloating, lower back pain, kidney and bladder problems, fibroids and cancer of the prostate gland, testicles, cervix or ovaries. Sexual dysfunction such as impotence, frigidity and infertility may develop.

Solar Plexus Chakra

The Solar Plexus chakra is situated just under the diaphragm and is the color yellow. This is the most corded chakra as it is the center for control, power and strength and is the chakra through which we tend to absorb other people's energies and issues. It therefore requires extra protection. The person who cords to the Solar Plexus of another usually wants to have power or control over that person and to affect their actions and behavior. Some cord to this chakra because they want you to be strong for them, stay and look after them and tell them what to do.

A cord here can force the chakra open and therefore make you far more vulnerable to other people's negativity. There may be issues of low self-esteem and lack of confidence, a loss of sense of individuality and personal freedom as well as problems connecting to and communicating appropriately with people. The individual may have feelings of confusion and self-doubt, powerlessness, worry, anxiety, fear, anger, resentment and even hatred. They may show a lack of will power, vitality, spontaneity and purpose.

In physical terms a cord to the Solar Plexus can lead to exhaustion, nausea, tension, bloating or pain in the abdomen. The Solar Plexus governs the liver, spleen, pancreas, stomach and digestive system. A cord may therefore cause problems in any or all of these organs including diabetes, ulcers, an inability to satisfy hunger, hypoglycemia, blood disorders, indigestion, irritable bowel, gall stones, abnormal metabolism, hypertension and lowered immune function.

Heart Chakra

The Heart chakra is located in the center of the chest and is traditionally green in color although some prefer to see it as pink. This chakra governs love, compassion, peace, joy and trust and is the bridge between our physical and spiritual aspects. A cord here is usually a positive one, but this needs to be checked as it could represent a one way demand of "nurture me," "love me" or "let me love you."

A negative cord at the Heart chakra can mean that you feel emotionally drained, tense, discontented, jealous, possessive and hold a fear of loss and perhaps anger towards yourself. There may be problems in relationships particularly with issues of trust, betrayal and self acceptance. Obsessive behavior or thoughts and an effect on the ability to give and receive love are also possible. This person is likely to be shy, lonely and isolated or bitter, critical and lacking compassion or love for themselves or others.

On a physical level a cord here may affect the corporeal heart, the lungs, circulatory system, arms and hands. So the victim might expect to experience palpitations, heart pain, coronary disease, high blood pressure, breathing problems such as asthma or even develop lung disease.

Throat Chakra

The Throat chakra is found in the neck and is the color of sky blue. It is the center for communication and links to the Sacral center for the expression of creativity and to the Heart for the expression of truth and wisdom. A cord here can indicate that you need the person to whom you are corded to speak for you or conversely that you want them to keep quiet so you can talk for them. This may come from shyness, lack of confidence or fear of speaking and a need for dependence upon another, but it can also be controlling, manipulative and involve forcing another person to express your negative views and even lies. The Throat center also governs our hearing and so the cord may mean "listen to me" or "let me listen on your behalf." A cord here may lead to problems in trusting others, giving and receiving, or feelings of betrayal and of not being heard or believed. It will probably affect the ability to freely express your truth and therefore block your creativity which in turn can soon lead to depression.

In physical terms a Throat cord can lead to hearing and speech difficulties. As this center is in the neck it can affect the thyroid gland, lead to a sore or swollen throat, a goiter or lump in the throat, plus tension and pain in the neck and shoulders, as well as mouth problems.

Brow Chakra

This chakra is located in the center of the forehead just above the top of the nose and is the color of indigo. The Brow chakra is associated with clairvoyance, intuition, self-awareness and imagination. A cord here can indicate a wish to interfere and intimidate you mentally and might impact on your thoughts, dreams, imagination and spiritual awareness. The opposite would be the demand that the corded person makes sense of life for you, thinks for you and tells you what to do and how to be.

A cord at the Brow can block this center or conversely ensure you are constantly psychically open and therefore vulnerable to intrusion. You may be subjected to telepathic thoughts, ideas, pictures, emotions, dreams or nightmares. You could have problems imagining, visualizing, meditating or working psychically and have constant thoughts of the person who is corded to you. There may be problems with memory and concentration and you might become confused, indecisive, disorientated, fearful and depressed.

On the physical side there can be problems with headaches and eyesight including loss of vision in extreme cases. The Brow chakra is connected with the pituitary, often described as the master gland, which governs the hormonal balance and metabolism of the body and if affected can cause weakness and weight loss, reproductive and kidney problems and diabetes. At the extreme end of the scale a Brow chakra cord could lead to brain disorders, learning difficulties including dyslexia and even hallucinations, delusions and schizophrenia.

Crown Chakra

This chakra is situated at the top of the head and is traditionally the color of violet, but is sometimes viewed as white or gold. It governs knowledge, understanding, wisdom, consciousness and spiritual connection. It is quite unusual to find a cord to this chakra, but if there is one the person doing the cording is very much intending to affect the victim's spiritual link. Someone may cord here to block, but also with the demand to receive teaching, spiritual information and wisdom.

A cord at the Crown chakra can cause the person to become isolated, alienated and disconnected from the world. They could become bored and apathetic with an inability to learn or absorb information. There might be telepathic communication and dreams sent by the person carrying out the cording. The victim would most likely experience problems in meditating, working spiritually and connecting with their God, Guides or Angels. There may be a lack of inspiration and grounding plus psychic invasion. This form of spiritual crisis can lead to confusion, despair, depression and suicidal thoughts.

In physical terms a cord at the Crown can cause the person to feel light headed and dizzy, have headaches and memory problems. The Crown center is linked with the pineal gland in the brain and if affected the person may experience sleeping, metabolism and immune system problems, neurological disorders and seizures. A cord here may also affect the cerebral cortex which governs the central nervous system as well as all of the higher human functions. At the extreme end senility or mental illness including psychosis may develop.

Cord Cutting

It is important to note that cord cutting does not harm either person or negatively affect any relationship or prevent the flow of unconditional love. On the contrary cord work can be very positive and lead to much healthier relationships. As we have seen above many cords affect us in very negative ways and do not allow us or the other person the freedom and flexibility to be our true selves. A cord creates vulnerability and reliance upon another to have our needs met when in effect we can and should learn to meet our own needs. Some people feel quite anxious about carrying out a cord cutting and this might indicate a dependent, collusive, obsessive or possessive relationship or issues such as guilt, the need for domination and power through manipulation and control, a sense of responsibility or duty, or the fear of having to be your own person and allowing the other partner their freedom. We are all aware of how painful an ending can be and in cases of divorce, abandonment or death any existing cord may be ripped out suddenly and this causes physical and emotional pain. People often describe it as being torn apart or feel as if something is missing, experiencing a sense of disorientation and disconnection. A cord cutting does not generally provide this experience as a cord is something that is usually unwanted. The work is planned, the issues understood and the removal is on an energetic level and at the appropriate pace.

There are many ways to cut cords and there is the capacity to be as creative as you wish. The key rule is that you must not harm the other person regardless of how angry or hurt you feel, even in a meditation or visualization. As we have discussed before thoughts are energy and can be transmitted and received through space and time. Any psychic attack you make on another person *will* rebound onto you.

Cord cutting if carried out with a clear intention can be very successful and rewarding. This work may be done alone or with assistance and even if the results are not immediate and the work has to be repeated there is no reason why at the end of the day you will not be free.

Practical Exercise

Make sure you are relaxed, grounded and protected in a bubble of white Light that is large enough to hold you and your energy field. Various methods for grounding and protection are covered in chapter 10. The first stage is to see or sense where the cord is attached to your body. If there is more than one cord work with the largest one first. The cord might be to a chakra, a limb, the torso or to an organ. Develop a sense of this cord and what it looks and feels like. Does it have a color? How thick is it? What is it made of? Look at or sense the other end of the cord and see who is there or who comes to mind. Perhaps you are surprised at who you see. Sense how this person seems. Are they angry, sad, calm, or surprised to be there? Surround this person in a bubble of Light to contain their energy. Note their reaction to this and if necessary tell them that they are not going to be harmed in any way. Notice where the cord is attached to them. If the cord runs between the chakras it is frequently the same chakra in each of you. If the cord is attached to a body part or organ for example, then the person at the other end may be holding it with their hands or have it tied around their waist.

Try to sense how long this cord has been there. Maybe since childhood or just for a few weeks. Does it feel as if it is still alive and vibrant, old or even dead? Develop a sense of the direction in which the energy in the cord is running. Is it running from you to them, them to you or flowing in both directions? If it is the latter does the energy run equally in either direction or more strongly one way? Get a sense of why this cord is there. What does it do and why are you cording to this person or them to you? What is each of you doing to encourage or accept this cord? Don't be afraid to take your time to achieve complete understanding.

If you wish, at this point you may have a conversation with the person to whom you are corded within your visualization. Decide what you would like to say to them. This might include the reason for cutting the cord and what you want from any future relationship between you. Once you have said all you need then listen to what they have to say in return. You might not receive any response at all or you may be surprised at what you are given. Decide what is needed to resolve any issues. Perhaps it is forgiveness, acceptance or an apology.

Now you need to find a method of cutting the cord between you and this may be at any point along the distance of the cord. You might decide to sever it with white Light or use scissors, a sword, knife, laser, fire, water or acid. Cut the cord at the point you have chosen so that it remains attached to each of you, but is separated. Starting with the part of the cord attached to you decide how you wish to destroy it. The only rule is not to bury the cord in the ground as it may have the opportunity to re-grow. You might decide to pull the cord out of you, burn or dissolve it. Make sure that all pieces of the cord are gone. If you have imagined burning it then get rid of the ashes. If you have symbolically dissolved it then make sure you have cleaned up any water, slime or other remains. One client worked with her Guide to destroy her cords and he would very helpfully arrive with a vacuum and clean up all the parts she pulled out. Some cords seem to have a plug on the end, many have roots, hooks or tentacles that entwine their way into the chakra or around the body or organ. You need to ensure you have removed all parts of the cord, even the pieces that may have lodged inside you.

The next stage is the cleansing of the affected parts of the body and chakra system. Imagine white Light pouring into the area that needs cleansing and sense this Light clearing out any tiny pieces of the cord or its residual energy. When you feel the area is really clean then it is important to fill the space. Some people actually feel an empty hole there. In spirit release work any void formed by the process must be filled to prevent something else using that space such as another cord or even an entity. Imagine pouring golden Light into the clean space left and know that this golden energy is healing that area and then sealing and protecting it. Once this is complete many people have a feeling of lightness and report that physical symptoms have vanished.

You must now do the same for the person on the other end of the cord. So first remove the cord and destroy it; cleanse with white Light and then fill, heal, seal and protect with the gold Light. Notice how they seem now. Many people at this point appear calm, relieved, happy and smiling.

If there are any other cords between you and this person they must be dealt with. If there is a positive Heart cord between you then it is acceptable to send and receive unconditional love through the cord. Once everything is complete you ensure that the other person is secure in their bubble of Light. You may wish to fill their bubble with a color or colors, with love, healing, forgiveness, hope, peace or joy. Allow them a few moments to absorb these qualities. The last part of the exercise is to send the image of that person in their bubble away into the Universe, watching until you can see them no longer. This separates your two energies allowing you both to be free. It also gives a message to your unconscious mind which works in images and pictures, that this severance has taken place and is complete. If as happens in a small number of cases, the person will not go out into the Universe, look at what is keeping them. Is there another cord that you have not spotted or is there something more to do or say before you can finally let them go?

Ensure that you too are surrounded in your bubble of Light and fill it with any color and qualities that you need. Make certain that you are grounded and have closed down and then allow yourself to come back gently.

Other Cord Cutting Methods

There are other forms of visualization which you may prefer such as standing in a nature scene, on a beach or in a field and burning the cords on a big bonfire, cleansing under a waterfall, sending the other person away in a hot air balloon, airplane or a boat, or imagining a vortex of white Light spinning around you to cut all cords and take them out into the Universe. If you are working with another person you can imagine seeing their cords in a large mirror or you might be able to feel them energetically with your hands. The essential parts of cord cutting are always to cut, cleanse, heal and protect the area.

If you are not a visual person then you can use salt water which is the Earth's great purifier. You could have a bath in which you dissolve a tablespoon of sea or rock salt or go swimming in the sea. The salt cleanses and protects both the physical and energetic bodies. Travel overseas can cut cords using the same principle of salt water. This latter method does not work with karmic cords which cannot be cut in this way. Crystal Clear essence available from Petaltone[8] can be sprayed over yourself, other people and objects or a few drops used in the bath to cleanse. The Petaltone essences of Golden Light, Clear Tone and Aura Flame are all designed to cut cords. Angelsword, an Australian Bush Flower essence, can be used to cut cords and clear psychic attack in general. A photograph of the person cording to you might be used with the phrase "I give back all that is yours and take back all that is mine."

Sometimes the cording may be coming through an object or photograph and if this persists after several attempts at cord cutting it might be sensible to dispose of the item. Competent use of a pendulum can be deployed to both find and clear cords. Certain crystals are good for cord cutting and may be placed on the chakra or relevant point on the body either with the intention of clearing the cord or it may be used as an energetic cutting tool. Clear quartz and selenite may be used for all cords, rose quartz for the Heart chakra, azurite for the Throat, moldavite for the Brow and a Herkimer diamond for the Base, Sacral, Solar Plexus, Heart and Throat chakras. If you prefer assistance with cutting your cords go to a healer who has experience in this type of work.

Conclusion

After cord cutting it is important not to allow yourself or the other person to re-cord. On an energetic level they will realize that a change has taken place even if they do not understand what has happened. They will invariably try to re-cord by telephoning or visiting you, often within twenty four hours of the cutting. Following workshops I have had participants contact me to say that after the de-cording the other person had phoned them hourly for two days or had suddenly arrived on the doorstep in the evening. You need to be aware of this possibility and use your protection techniques (see chapter 10), your intention and persistence to prevent a re-cording. If they do manage to re-cord to you then use a de-cording technique as soon as possible. It is perfectly possible to continue a relationship with someone while not allowing a cord to form between you. In fact it is much healthier as mentioned previously. If however, you want the cord to reform - it will do so.

You will notice that after cutting the cords the energy between the two of you will change. If there has been anger or guilt before you will find that this is diminished and easier to deal with positively. If one of you has had more control and power than the other you will find that this becomes more balanced. Cutting cords leads to change especially in behavior. If someone has always been very demanding towards you they might not stop this behavior in the short term, but due to the cord cutting your way of coping with them and their demands will have altered in a positive way. When an alteration takes place within us other people often desperately try to make us change back, to reinstate the status quo from their point of view. It is up to you to take responsibility for the positive changes in your behavior and needs and to communicate those clearly. We can only ever transform ourselves and sometimes altering our behavior, views and attitudes effects a positive change in others. That demanding, angry parent who used to regularly cause you tears might respond to your changed behavior after the cord cutting by being more gentle and less difficult. There are of course no guarantees!

CHAPTER FOUR
INTENTIONAL PSYCHIC ATTACK

In this chapter we will be looking at witchcraft, black magic, Vodou and curses. These terms are generally used when the psychic attack on a person or property is intentional with the expectation of a harmful outcome. It is important to note here that Vodou (also spelled Voudou/Voodoo) is a religion just as Christianity and Buddhism are religions. The word Vodou has drawn a negative connotation over time as people generally use this term to denote a practice which has a harmful result. As with any other practice using energy and intention, Vodou can be used either positively or negatively.

Witchcraft and magic can also be separated into the "white" and "black" arts. White magic is usually defined as working with nature in order to help and heal. Black magic is the use of dark occult forces for self gain, power and control. The word occult is often taken to be negative in meaning, but in fact means hidden or invisible and therefore applies to all energy work. There is always choice as to whether to use the occult, a belief or ritual, witchcraft, magic or healing energies for positive or negative ends. I have worked with a number of clients who have experienced "healers" who are psychic vampires. I have also met clients who have been taken in by energy workers who coerce and manipulate, often using the power of hypnotic suggestion in order to extract large sums of money from their victim. A few clients have found themselves in a cult, sometimes for many years before realizing the situation and then had great difficulty in escaping.

Today we can openly purchase books on magic and witchcraft from high street shops to the extent of some selling "Vodou dolls" complete with pins. Even in "white" magic or witchcraft there are for example, various love potions, spells and rituals designed to make another person fall in love with you. To my mind this is manipulation of another person to meet your own wishes and is probably not in their best interests or yours. It is in fact a form of psychic attack which may have karmic repercussions for you both.

In my view we can only work on ourselves or someone else with the appropriate permission and for the highest good of each. This is how any form of healing works and students are taught not to attach themselves to a specific outcome when working with clients. Any meditation, visualization, magic or ritual should therefore retain the focus of respect for the other person and their process. You cannot make someone fall in love with you, but you can work on loving yourself and radiating love and positive energy so that people are naturally more attracted towards you. In the same way you can work on manifesting more money and a better job by working on yourself and in trusting the Universe to provide whatever you need. You do not have to attempt to energetically control or manipulate your boss to give you a pay rise or promotion.

Anyone carrying out an intentional psychic attack means to cause harm to their victim. It could be that the attacker is jealous or angry and wants to make you feel bad too. Their intention might be more specific and could include wanting to stop your relationship with someone, or a business enterprise. The attacker perhaps wants to control your actions or thoughts, your ability to have a partner or children, your happiness or wealth. They may wish to make you unwell or in the extreme to end your life. These attacks can be formed by thought alone or might come through equipment such as telephones and computers. Water and electricity are both excellent carriers of psychic energy. In serious cases of psychic attack I have had to clean and protect all the water and electricity inlets into the client's house to prevent continued contamination. One very effective method of doing this is to visualize white Light filters at all appropriate external points. The filters then allow positive electricity and water into the house, but remove all negative energies.

Thought Forms

Thought forms are literally energetic shapes created by repetitive, focused, strong thoughts which may be psychically seen, felt or sensed in the aura. We create our own thought forms as we progress through life and many are initiated in childhood by parents, guardians or teachers. If as a child you were persistently told you were stupid or bad, would never amount to anything, were not creative or no good at math then you might develop a thought form in your energy field that holds that verbal instruction. If as an adult you continue to believe this programming and put energy into it you will carry on reinforcing it. You might even say and believe such things as "I'm not creative," "I'm no good with money," "everything I do goes wrong" or "I'll never be successful." Sometimes the thought form holds an emotion such as fear or anger which may have been caused by an event or various experiences.

Such emotions help to strengthen the thoughts and beliefs held. To me these types of thought form appear in the aura as a two dimensional dark shape. I frequently find them in people's energy fields and by sensing the thought form can often repeat to the client what instruction or energy it holds.

Thought forms act as blocks in life and can hold you back. They can prevent you from applying for certain jobs because "I'm not good enough" or from developing certain relationships because "people won't like me." The key to dealing with any thought form is to first assess whether you actually believe the maxim because often you don't. I used to believe I am not creative because I am not good at producing artistic drawings. However, I am creative in my work and with money, words, time, projects and ideas. So I decided to stop saying and thinking that I'm not creative which is immensely freeing. If you believe you are not good at something you feel deficient in some way. This may lead to feelings of guilt, shame or even jealousy of those who can do something you feel you cannot. We can't all be brilliant at the same things and it is important to recognize the actions and qualities in which we do excel and be free to admire the achievements of others.

If you find that you do not actually agree with the thought form you are carrying then you are half way there. Even if you have operated within that negative energy for many years it is never too late to change. The first step is to turn your thoughts into positive ones. So start saying and believing "I am creative," "I am loved," "I am confident," "I am a good parent" or whatever is relevant to you. Once you have accepted that the negative thought form exists and perhaps even understand why it is there and where or who it came from you can decide to change your thoughts and behavior and therefore change your feelings too.

The next part of the process is to release the thought form. You may do this by imagining it disappearing or by cutting the cord holding it to you as described in the previous chapter. You might decide to imagine submerging the thought form in water or surrounding it in white Light to cleanse and dissolve it. You may choose to use fire which, just as in the Phoenix rising from the ashes, acts as a cleanser and transforms any negative energy into positive energy. Another alternative is to put the thought form into a bag or box for easy transportation and then ask your Angels or Guides to come and collect it. Find a method that suits you using the creativity which you now recognize you have!

Past Life Thought Forms

The concept of past lives is familiar to many people. Time however, is not linear and there is more than just this one dimension of time and space. Put simply therefore, a "past life" may actually be a future life or even a co-existence in a parallel dimension. When I refer to past lives throughout this book for the sake of simplicity, it may be more accurate to consider "other" lives.

We can also hold thought forms of other life events in our energy field or corporeal body. This type of thought form frequently appears three dimensional and gives an indication of the events of that other lifetime. For example, I have seen knives, spears and arrows that have previously caused the person's death, protruding from a part of their body. I have often seen chains and manacles around the neck, wrists and ankles indicating a life of slavery or imprisonment. Others have been hung as seen by the noose still around their neck. The interesting issue here is that in this lifetime the person will often have a mark on the body or a pain or weakness where the weapon has been and when it is removed will notice a difference. Those with chains around their ankles may have had great difficulty in moving forward in this lifetime always feeling that something has been holding them back. Those who were previously hanged may have throat problems or even been born into this life with the umbilical cord around their neck.

The aura and the physical body right down to cellular level retain the memories of the past. Fortunately we do not hold onto all of our other life experiences or we would be weighed down by all sorts of thought forms. It is generally the particularly strong, traumatic memories or feelings from other lives, those which have not yet been resolved that cause an imprint to establish itself. This imprint in the manifestation of a thought form can be seen clairvoyantly. A thought form might also be created through a traumatic experience from the current lifetime. It may even be one that has been transferred down through the generations of a family for example, "our family always has bad luck."

In order to remove this type of other life thought form it is important to acknowledge the issues raised. For example, someone who has committed suicide through hanging in another time may still have suicidal thoughts in this life. Sometimes this is because they are repeating previous patterns and heading perhaps toward the same outcome. This person requires ongoing healing and counseling to ensure that they have time to look at and understand those patterns and make any necessary changes. On the other hand it may be that the energy of the thought form is strong enough in itself to promote suicidal ideation. In this case the energetic removal of the noose from the person's throat may lead to a cessation of thoughts about ending their life.

The removal of the imprinted image can be done simply and quickly by pulling the sword from the back or gently lifting the noose or umbilical cord from around the neck. Healing of the physical and emotional wounds needs to take place. It is important to tell the body that it no longer has to remember this traumatic event of the past, but can now move forward into the future unencumbered. This does not have to be done by speaking aloud, but can be just as effective carried out in silent thought.

Thought Forms Used in Psychic Attack

Psychic attack frequently employs thought forms. As we have seen before, psychic attack is not always intentional. In the same way the actual thought form created may not be intentional, but is produced by the desire to affect someone. For example, I worked with a man who was recently divorced and having problems with his ex-wife. He claimed he was under psychic attack from her. Apparently his wife was extremely angry with him and expressed this anger towards him mentally and also verbally. When I tuned into his energy I psychically saw he was wearing a chastity belt. When I told him this the man stated he had been impotent since their separation some time before. He then admitted that the separation and subsequent divorce was due to the fact that he had been unfaithful to his wife. In this case his ex-wife may not have actually thought of locking him in a chastity belt, but had clearly wished that his sexual activity and drive were affected. Her intense anger and the focused mental thoughts had created what I recognized as an implement used in medieval times to prevent women from having sexual intercourse while their husbands were away from home.

Common thought forms seen in psychic attack scenarios include knives in the back and we've all heard the common expression "stab in the back." I frequently see razor blades and nails in the stomach and intestines. The latter as you can imagine may cause severe pain and digestive problems. I know of several people who have been taken to the Accident and Emergency Department of their local hospital with violent stomach pains and vomiting and nothing has been physiologically wrong with them. After many tests and X-rays the doctors are baffled and send them home. Once the psychic attack has been dealt with by removing the offending thought forms the abdominal problems cease. It should be noted here that a cord to the Solar Plexus can also cause abdominal pain and nausea. Cutting the cord as described in the previous chapter can also end the abdominal distress.

One young woman with whom I worked had been married for three years to a man she loved very much. She used to be very healthy and vibrant before they met and held a responsible job. Her health started to decline when they decided to become engaged and she was at the point when seeing me of being so sick and frail that she could no longer work. Doctors were unable to find a cause for her ill health and weakness until an enlightened private doctor abroad told her that she was under psychic attack.

When I tuned into this client's energy I saw behind her a dark haired woman who I described to her. She told me that I had described her mother-in-law. I sensed from the mother-in-law that she did not want my client as a daughter-in-law and felt she was not good enough for her son. The young woman confirmed this. After sending the mother-in-law away and carrying out some protection with the young woman I looked into her physical body. I saw razor blades and bent nails in her digestive system plus a uterine coil. It became clear that not only did the mother-in-law want to affect her daughter-in-law's health, but was also stopping her from producing children. As I tuned into the uterine device I heard "if she doesn't have children my son will leave her." This was clearly a case of intentional attack and I discovered that the mother-in-law knew a great deal about black magic.

Unfortunately in family situations it is easy to attack using objects. In this case there were obviously family photos, gifts exchanged, visits to the home and food prepared, all of which can be used in intentional psychic attack. The young woman and I did some sessions to work with this complex attack and she started to get better. Her husband was unable to accept that his mother would do such things to her, but remained very supportive of his wife and both attended one of my workshops on the subject.

There is a method in which an object can be used to stop a psychic attack. You send something that is one hundred percent cotton tied in a red cotton thread or ribbon to your supposed attacker. This technique is apparently of African origin and was used successfully by the client of a colleague. Unfortunately the client was not sure who had been sending the attacks and so sent out a hundred cotton tea towels tied with red ribbon to potential suspects. Suffice to say the attacks stopped, but she still did not know the culprit. As this method needs to be repeated annually she continues to send out a hundred cotton tea towels at Christmas time!

Witchcraft, Black Magic And Vodou

Having looked at thought forms and cords I now turn to the black occult arts which also utilize for example, possessions, images, body fluids, nails and hair in order to harm another person. Much of this work is ritualistic, but does not have to be. Focused thought is actually all that is required in order to attack and also to repel an assault. I believe in giving people information that empowers them in dealing safely with the occult arts. I cannot warn you strongly enough that this information must not be used in a negative way.

When someone comes to me because they think they are under attack I carry out an assessment of their energy. In doing this I can usually verify if an attack has taken place and if the attacks are still continuing. I frequently see and am able to describe the person carrying out the attacks. Sometimes it is a person known to the client and in some cases this may be of considerable surprise to them. Occasionally it is not a person that the client recognizes.

It needs to be borne in mind that it is also possible for the client to produce a thought form of the person they think is attacking them. For example, let's assume that Elizabeth thinks Jane is psychically attacking her. Elizabeth becomes angry or fearful and often thinks about Jane and the psychic attack. Quite quickly she creates a thought form of Jane in her aura. In manifesting this thought form Elizabeth may also create her own psychic attack symptoms in effect attacking herself. An experienced healer is able to tell the difference between the client's created thought form and the clairvoyant image of a genuine attacker in someone's energy field. A real person and a created thought form have a different feel to them. The first feels real, alive and with a consciousness whereas a thought form does not generally have all these qualities.

In the hypothetical example of Elizabeth and Jane an experienced healer would be able to discern whether Jane is actually carrying out a psychic attack on Elizabeth and stop it from continuing. If Jane is innocent and Elizabeth has created a thought form there are two options. Either the true attacker is discovered and dealt with or Elizabeth needs to acknowledge what she has done and stop attacking herself.

On one occasion I had a young woman referred to me by a sensitive who had seen a symbolic carved wooden figure in front of her. When I described the woman who had carried out the attack some time before, the client initially said she did not know her. As I worked to remove the symbol she remembered that the woman I had described had become agitated while they were both waiting in a shop queue. She did not appear to like my client even though they had not spoken to each other. The woman had sent out the thought form of a protective African symbolic figure which was now in my client's auric field. In this one-off brief meeting the woman in the queue had obviously felt threatened in some way by my client. Instead of putting up a protective barrier around herself she had sent an image of protection to the client who had then unconsciously held onto it. The block was easily removed and the client got on with her life.

Sometimes the person I see is not recognizable to the client because they have been paid by a third party to carry out a piece of work. In this case I may see the triangular relationship of my client, the paid attacker or witch doctor, plus the person paying for the attack to take place. In situations of a paid attack then it may be a one-off assault with long term effects. On the other hand I may find that the energy has gone from the original attack, but the person remains blocked in moving forward in their life. In this case the attack has caused a thought form which has not naturally dispersed. In some cases the attack is an old one which has dead energy with it and is not particularly affecting the client now, but is found by chance during a regular healing session and just needs clearing.

People who pay others to carry out a psychic attack often do so because they feel they do not have the skill or knowledge necessary. Others pay someone because they feel that their involvement will not be found out and if anything rebounds it won't be onto them. They are wrong. Even if they are not discovered by someone like me their deed is known spiritually and it will rebound karmically. They are also caught in the triangular relationship with the attacker and the victim as mentioned above. Triangles are very powerful as each person involved has some form of relationship with the other two. Each of the three people is locked into the dynamic of the triangle.

An example of this is a woman in her late thirties who came to see me stating emphatically that she had been under attack from her sister in America for the last fifteen years. She felt that this attack had caused her poor health, she had been unable to keep a job or to conceive children and more recently her husband had divorced her. The client had been trying to stop the attacks for some time without success. When I tuned into her energy I immediately saw a black man who was not at all pleased to see me. He started sending all sorts of symbols and various types of attack towards me and the client. Fortunately, as I always work with powerful protection and had instantly been able to create a very strong barrier, he could not reach us. I found that he was on the island of Haiti where I discovered later a particularly dark, potent and specialist form of Vodou is practiced by the Bokor. The Bokor is a practitioner who will use his skills for both healing as well as attack. I saw a link between him and my client, but also with her sister who was paying him on a regular basis to continue the attacks. My client did not recognize the Haitian Vodou practitioner as she had never met him, but she did recognize her sister when described.

This was a very powerful triangle with the sister strongly bound to the Haitian man through her regular payments which he had grown to expect. It appeared that every six months she would fly to Haiti to visit him and seemed to be understandably frightened of him. He was bound to my client because she was the reason for his continued income. The sister had issues of jealousy and competition with my client who was in turn angry and professed hatred for her sister. These strong emotions obviously held the triangle together in a very powerful way. I worked to cut the links of the three sides of the triangle and to prevent the Bokor from carrying out any further attacks. There was a contract in place between him and the sister which also had to be terminated. Contracts will be looked at in detail in chapter 8. In all cases I send healing to the attacker and the person making the payment and usually involve the client in doing so. In this case however, my client was adamant that she did not want to send healing to her sister so I completed the work without her involvement.

This case also raises the very important issue of rebound or kick back. On psychically linking into the witch doctor in Haiti he immediately realized that I had discovered him and attacked. In this work we need to be very aware that professional and intentional attackers are often experts in their art and will know when anyone connects with their energy in any way. If you are unable to protect and defend yourself sufficiently you may be severely affected by their reaction. I have met several very skilled occultists practicing the dark arts who have attempted to attack and stop me from carrying out my work. Ultimately my awareness of my powerful protection, my lack of fear, the fact that I never work without my team of Light Beings and therefore my absolute knowing that I am stronger than the attacker means that I have never been seriously affected. Each assailant I have met in this way has eventually withdrawn from the confrontation.

If you are attempting to stop a psychic attack an awareness of rebound is essential. One of my students was being regularly attacked by a very skilled occultist and she decided to retaliate by psychically sending hot lava to him. The instant she did so he retaliated by reflecting it back. The sensation of hot lava surrounded and filled her body. This took her some time to deal with until the burning stopped and she learned a very valuable lesson. The first rule of defense is to stop and not to harm the assailant. It is only very occasionally that an attacker has been so persistent that I have been given permission by my Guides to return the attack to them. This invariably stops the aggressor, but should not be carried out lightly and without spiritual permission or there is the possibility of instant or karmic rebound.

Sometimes a psychic attack is carried out by a group of people and this can produce a strong, continuous assault. This type of group either meets regularly in order to reinforce the harassment or establishes a program which is self-running. Even group energy can be stopped, but your energy must be strong and consistent and it may take some time.

In any attack if you clear the negative energy, but expect the assault to continue then your expectation allows it to do so. Just as if you expect your protection to fail or feel that it isn't good enough then it won't be. People will cleanse and protect themselves and then think "I wonder if that has worked?" The doubt and fear you hold will weaken your protection and resistance to continued psychic attack. Positive thoughts and affirmations such as "I do not accept any negative energy/psychic attack" are much more effective.

Body Parts and Products

So let us look then at the use of various types of attack. As mentioned earlier intentional attackers frequently use body fluids and products. In the past chickens would be bricked into a building either alive or dead, sometimes along with shoes and candlesticks to ward off evil spirits. People would also bury witch bottles in the foundations or walls, or under the hearth or threshold of their houses to protect the occupants against witchcraft. These witch bottles were used between the sixteenth and nineteenth centuries to stop or return spells to the witch or even kill her. They were most common in the seventeenth century at the height of the witch hunts in Britain. Witch bottles were usually filled with urine, hair and bent iron nails or pins to cause pain or they were heated on a fire to cause burning until the spell was removed. Sometimes the bottles would contain bones, thorns, spiky grass and pieces of wood or fabric. The bottles often had the face of the witch etched into the neck of the stoneware bottle and were thrown into the river or buried in the ground. If the witch was not known to the person believing they were under attack the bottle would be set and they would wait for one of their neighbors or family to suddenly become ill or die. Unfortunately the probably innocent person would then be branded a witch.

Body parts or products hold the essence of the individual and are therefore very powerful. Many people are now aware of muti magic following the discovery of the torso of five year old "Adam" in the River Thames in London in 2001. Muti is a South African word which means traditional medicine. Various herbs and animal parts are used by the African sangomas, the traditional healers, to help and heal people. More recently however muti has become known to be used in a negative occult way. The belief is that humans have stronger energies than the more traditional herbs and animals. Children have an even more powerful energy as they are innocent and uncontaminated. "Adam" is thought to be the victim of a muti murder where particular body parts are taken, usually while the person is still alive and screaming, in order to enhance the potency of the medicine. There are other examples of children being taken from their villages, the genitals removed and the child returned to their village, if they are "fortunate" enough not to be left in the bush to die. The body parts may be used in potions, smeared onto the body, eaten, or used as a talisman – all with the desire of achieving better health, fortune or prospects.

Different cultures across the globe use body parts and products, usually of animals, but I have also seen human parts. When I tune into someone who is being attacked and see the perpetrator I frequently see the method which has been used to carry out the attack. This is very useful because if you know how it has been done you can undo it. So for example, if I see knotted string I carefully untie each knot releasing the intention it holds. If I see a symbol in place in the aura of the victim or in the home I then ask to be shown how it was drawn. I carefully note down where the drawing of the symbol was started and where completed. I then quite simply draw it backwards with my finger in the air or in my mind to erase it. This is a straight forward way to deal with an easy symbol such as the pentagram or five sided star. The most difficult one I ever saw looked just like an electrical circuit board which would have taken hours and much concentration to trace backwards, but one of my Guides easily and very helpfully completed the task in a matter of minutes.

A woman of Indian origin came to see me saying she was under attack. When I tuned into her I saw a small white building of just one room, a doorway and no windows. On this occasion I used the technique of astral projection to travel to the building. Astral projection or travel is the projection of consciousness or a stepping out of the physical body to travel with the astral body. During astral projection I retain all of my physical senses. Sometimes I simply carry out a remote viewing which is an ability to accurately see what is happening elsewhere without leaving the body. Both methods allow you to review what has happened before the present time – in effect time travel.

I entered the room and saw a black iron symbol on the wall facing me and to my right in the corner was a large pot full of a dark liquid. I sensed that the room was somewhere in Mauritius and asked what I needed to do first. My Guides informed me that I needed to deal with the pot in order to undo the most potent part of the spell. As I emptied the foul smelling pot I was expecting to find animal parts which I duly did. The dark liquid was chicken blood mixed with various other ingredients. Chickens and their blood are very commonly used in witchcraft, Vodou and black magic. In my astral state I found a chopped up baby goat which I took back to its whole state and buried it. The most horrifying thing I found in the pot was the hands and feet of a human baby. As I traced backwards in time I discovered that they had been taken from an almost full term stillborn baby boy who had then been buried. I was only slightly relieved by the fact that at least the baby had apparently died of natural causes before it was mutilated. I reunited his hands and feet with his body and gave healing to the child and his mother. This was potent magic and as I worked I was aware that I had not only the protection of my Guides, but of a figure that my client later told me was one of the Hindu Goddesses. Having emptied and destroyed the pot I removed the symbol on the wall by retracing it. I then cleansed the room itself.

On informing the client what I had seen and carried out she confirmed that she had an aunt in Mauritius who she suspected was carrying out the attack. She was also aware that animals such as goats and chickens and sometimes parts of dead babies were used in this type of ritual. After this session the attacks on my client ceased.

I have also worked with many people where body products have played a large part in the attack against them. Sometimes the attacker has used their own body parts or fluids to influence the victim. One client stayed in a "friend's" house and when she went to bed felt really uncomfortable. She subsequently became quite distressed when she felt as if there was something in the room attacking her. She noticed that there was a bowl under a dresser containing a liquid that appeared to be urine. At this point deciding to flee she left the house in the middle of the night. In this case the presence of the urine would indicate some form of intentional interference by the "friend" and there were possibly other things hidden in the room as well. Fortunately she didn't stay to find out what they might be.

In other instances the attacker's body products such as urine, faeces, menstrual blood, semen, hair, ground finger or toe nails may be used in the victim's food or drink. More common is the use of these body fluids or parts belonging to the victim. Either way this effectively creates a psychic link between the attacker and their victim. These products may be formed into a potion, used in a ritual, burned, incorporated into an image of the person to stab with pins or any other methods all with the intention of harming or controlling the victim.

One woman took the semen of her partner and sent it to a witch doctor in Africa. When he left her and started a relationship with another woman with whom he wanted children, they found after a couple of years of trying that they were unable to conceive. They both went for the usual tests and it was found that his sperm count was virtually nil and those that did exist were completely malformed. When he came to me for help aware of what his previous partner had done I saw that the African witch doctor had very successfully used the collected semen to affect his fertility. Despite trying to reverse this it had taken effect so well over a period of two or three years that the attempts of myself and the client were unsuccessful.

The effects of psychic attack using body parts or fluid can often be dissolved by disempowering what was taken and by psychically undoing the ritual or potion and destroying anything created such as a doll used to torture the victim. Just as intention has been used to create the attack then your intention is essential to un-create it. It is often advisable to find out the reason for the attack which I do by sensing the energy held or by having a telepathic conversation with the attacker. Of course, there is no guarantee that the attacker will want to talk to me so sometimes the conversation is one way! In all cases of attack I send healing to the attacker after disarming and disempowering whatever was used. In most cases I will telepathically advise the assailant that any further attacks are forbidden and sometimes talk to them about karmic effects. I have found on this latter point that many intentional and often professional attackers have no interest in what might rebound onto them later. They are only interested in short term gains and what is happening now and many seem to think they are so powerful that they are immune from karmic repercussions. Only in extreme circumstances and with permission from the Beings of Light should you use binding to contain an attacker in some way. In all cases of psychic attack after removing and disempowering the negative effects I carry out a healing and protection of the client.

Objects

Objects such as gifts exchanged between attacker and victim, jewelry, clothes and photos can all be used to create a psychic link between two or more people. We have already mentioned jewelry in relation to psychic vampires and cording. Jewelry can also be programmed with an intention to harm, control, bring bad luck or whatever the attacker intends. Each time the jewelry is worn the cumulative effect increases. It is therefore important to cleanse your jewelry regularly just as you would cleanse your physical and energy bodies. We will be looking at cleansing and protection techniques in chapter 10. The same effects can be realized through clothing which may also be contaminated by sewing small objects which have been magically empowered into the seams or hem.

When I visit houses in order to clear them I frequently come across ornaments, figurines, pots and so on that have a negative energy with them. Sometimes this energy has been created at the same time as the object. For example, a man makes a carved wooden figure while furious about an argument he had with his wife that morning. The finished item is likely to hold some of his anger within it and can therefore carry that to the new owner of the carving. Some objects have not been contaminated at the time of creation, but afterwards by someone who had an intention to adversely affect the recipient of their gift. Many of these objects can be cleared, but a few have to be destroyed. Burning is a good option or wrapping the article in black plastic and taking it to the local refuse dump. My plea here is that if you think you have an object in your house which is holding negative energy do not take it to the local charity shop or give it to a friend. All you are doing is passing on the negative energy which does not tend to discriminate who it affects. Karmically this is not responsible behavior.

If someone has an object belonging to you or one that you have given them which is being used to attack then it may be possible to retrieve it or to disempower it through cleansing. Cleansing may be carried out using your intention and visualization perhaps using white Light or water. You do not need to have contact with the object in order to cleanse it.

Scrying is a very ancient and legitimate method of clairvoyance utilized to foresee events. The scryer might use a mirror, a bowl of water or a crystal ball. Unfortunately this facility may also be used with malevolent intention. Mirrors can be used by an attacker to both send attacks and to view their victim at will. This includes mirrors of all sizes including those that are freestanding, fixed to a wall and even small make up mirrors. A mirror that has been tampered with in this way will distort your image when you look into it. You may even be able to glimpse movement or figures deep within the glass. The mirror in effect has become a gateway and may be dealt with as described in chapter 6. All gateways need to be cleansed, closed and then sealed. If you feel unable to do this then cover the mirror until you are able to have it cleared.

Photographs are very powerful. In some cultures people do not allow photographs to be taken of themselves because they are aware that the picture holds to some extent their personal essence. Some authors do not allow a photo of themselves to appear in their book to prevent people identifying, attacking or cording to them. I often have clients who bring or send me photos to facilitate healing work. It is quite simple to psychically sense a range of information from a picture. This can be done either by looking directly at it or by holding it between the hands and reading it psychometrically. In group shots you may pick out those who are deceased. You can sense whether the person pictured has negative energy around them or even has a spirit attached. It is also possible to carry out for example, a whole reading of their character, personality and lifestyle. If an attacker wants to affect their victim through a photograph it is quite simple to use it in a ritual, to deface or damage it in some way or to work purely with the intention of bringing harm. Just as with any other object the photograph can be cleansed to prevent the attacks from continuing. You might want to imagine the picture surrounded in white Light or ask your Guides, Angels or Ascended Masters to cleanse and protect it from further abuse.

As you can see, in cases of a family member attacking others within the family which is more common than you might imagine, the ability to both provide and gain access to gifts, photographs, food, drink, clothing, houses and so on is enormous. In one instance the victim of a fairly complex attack had a key ring that belonged to their female assailant. The client agreed to send me the key ring and I sat with it and tuned into its owner. The assailant and I had a long telepathic conversation and I showed her that I had her key fob. She was very aware of the power of holding an object belonging to someone as she had used various methods herself involving clothing, food, gifts, and photos. Since that time she immediately ended her attacks while I have continued to hold onto the key ring to ensure that she does not renew her efforts.

Entities

Unfortunately some practitioners of the dark arts summon various entities to attack their victims. Some of these entities are merely thought forms and will therefore appear as two dimensional. This type of entity may have a consciousness albeit limited. When speaking with a thought form entity it will be restricted in what it can tell you and may repeat stock phrases. It has no concept of right and wrong and its function is to carry out instructions. When asked why it is here it may repeat that it wants to harm or destroy the victim, but will not be able to explain why. It does however, acknowledge that it has been sent and by whom and when asked if it would like to return to its master or creator will often readily agree. In this way it is quite easily dispatched. Sometimes it might be preferable to remove and dissolve it as a thought form without returning it to the creator. Through asking for guidance and permission I am made aware of the most appropriate course of action in each case.

It is important to realize that occasionally the entities summoned and sent to the victim are actually the attacker's own darkness or what Carl Jung called Shadow. Within all of us are the dualities of light and dark, positive and negative in differing quantities. The Universal Law of duality or polarity relates to the necessity for opposites such as love and hate, joy and sorrow, masculine and feminine, yin and yang. The Universal Law of balance is brought into play to achieve harmony between them. Many Light or energy workers are striving to increase their Light or positive energy and this involves work on our darkness or Shadow side. The Shadow holds our demons and wounds which may include negative emotions, difficult experiences from the past and the aspects of ourselves that we do not like. We cannot fully eradicate our Shadow side, but we can come to terms with it and hold an awareness of when we are projecting the contents of our Shadow onto other people. These projections may become thought forms and hold a strong energy especially if the attacker is more focused on their dark, negative aspects than their positive qualities. This type of thought form is dealt with in the same way as with any other created thought or energy.

In other instances the assailant may summon one of the Dark Force Entities (DFE's) or demons or perhaps elemental spirits, all of which will be covered in greater depth in chapters 5 and 8.

These are not quite so easy to deal with although again they may be happy to return to the person that summoned them and to whom they relate as their master. They do have a consciousness and therefore may be more amenable to communication, but are less open to negotiation or instruction. Summoning a negative spirit to do work for you is never a good idea and it may even become attached to you. This invariably draws you into dimensions and agreements that you may later seriously regret. It is not an area to play with and you can never guarantee what it is that will respond to your summons. This is why many people experience problems using an Ouija Board still sold in some shops today as a game. Even if you call upon a Guide, an Angel or an Ascended Master you still need to check out whether it is actually one of these Light Beings which has arrived and not a Shape Shifter or any other form of entity that pretends to be something which it is not. To find out more about this refer to chapter 9.

Curses

Curses are interesting because they mostly rely upon the belief of the curser and/or the cursed. Usually curses are empowered by both thought and emotion. Many of you will have had the experience of being offered the purchase of "lucky" heather on the street. If you decided not to buy it you may have heard the seller mutter or even shout something after you as you walked away. In all probability this was not a wish for your good health and fortune. Many people have a fear of people such as travelers or gypsies thinking that they are experts in the occult. After all everyone has seen or heard of the gypsy fortune tellers who read palms and crystal balls. So as you walk away from the heather seller do you enter into fear and assume that what was muttered was a curse? If you believe in the ability of that person to place a curse upon you then you immediately give away your power to him/her and dive into self-fulfilling expectation. You expect disaster to strike which heightens your anxiety and means that you are more likely to do something a bit rash. If you subsequently fall over, step out in front of a bus or lose some money then the supposed "curse" has worked. You can then blame the gypsy for your misfortune and continue to live in fear of the effects of the "curse."

On the other hand if you leave the heather seller and ignore the muttering, refusing to allow this brief encounter to affect you, then you will almost certainly be fine. You remain relaxed and therefore less likely to have an accident or make a mistake of some kind. As we discovered earlier all psychic attack ultimately depends on you allowing the attack to affect you.

If someone is intending to harm you and is skilful in doing so then of course they may have an effect on you if you are not effectively protected or self-aware. If you are aware of your energy and any changes to your wellbeing then you can deal with any attack as soon as possible. You may be aware of an attack as it comes towards you and before it fully enters your energy field, body or environment. In this case you can send it away into the Universe asking for any negative energy to be transmuted into positive energy. If the attack has entered your energy field then you need to deal with it before it has a chance to take hold. It is much easier to remove negative energy or even a spirit attachment which has been there two weeks rather than one that has been there for two years. If you feel unable to deal with this yourself then find a healer or psychic who can help you. Cleansing techniques will be covered in more detail in chapter 10.

A very simple example given to me some years ago by a psychology tutor may be of use here. If someone throws you a ball you have a choice. You could catch it in which case you then have to deal with it. So for example, you could try to throw it back, hold onto it or put it back where it belongs. In this scenario you have to take responsibility for what to do with the ball next. Your alternative is to not catch the ball and perhaps let it hit you and fall away from you or you could simply move aside so it goes straight past. You have not therefore accepted the ball from the other person and it remains their problem as to how to deal with it. Do they have to chase and continue to look after it or put it away? Or do they just walk away as well? If someone sends you a psychic attack you ultimately have the same choices.

Some people become caught up in the glamour or drama of the curse or other forms of psychic attack. They blame the curse or their attacker and continue to go round in circles of self-fulfilling expectation and bad luck. A woman came to me with a long written list of people who had supposedly cursed or attacked her in some way dating back for the last thirty years. She blamed these people for all of the problems she had experienced in her life which admittedly were many. At no point did she accept any responsibility for the choices she had made regarding partners, sexual behavior, lifestyle, education, employment or diet. The woman complained of a large weight gain in the last three years blaming the psychic attacks and the spirits she claimed were with her. On assessment of her energy I found no spirit attachment or any curses, thought forms, cords or symbols. In effect no psychic attack of any kind. When we looked at her diet we established that it consisted of all the foods which we are constantly advised not to eat. In addition the client would often comfort eat several bars of chocolate in one sitting. This eating pattern appeared to have been initiated by the death of her mother three years previously which had affected her terribly and for whom she was still grieving. The reasons for her weight gain became very clear.

Over the years she had been constantly obsessed with the idea of occult forces attacking her, reading and thinking about it and writing tomes on her computer about her experiences. This client had also visited various healers and psychics in an attempt to remove the spirits and the curses. She found it extremely difficult to talk about her present life or health apart from her weight gain, as she was fixated in the past. My work with her was mainly healing, counseling and encouraging her to think of the current and future possibilities for herself. She found it hard to understand that by constantly dwelling on the past negative aspects of her life that she was in effect holding onto them and the energy they held and therefore continuing her state of affairs. This is a sad, but not uncommon scenario for many people who get caught up in being "special" through claiming psychic attack.

So having looked at how a curse generally operates let's now look at the type of curses that exist. A curse is simply a wish to cause harm which can be carried out by thought, verbally or through ritual. Usually the curse is made once with sufficient intention to cause it to continue over a period of time. Some curses however, may be reinforced at regular intervals or a program formulated to maintain their operation.

The person who creates a curse or causes any other form of psychic attack is usually very interested in how their victim is faring. If you meet them they may regularly ask how you are or how your business is doing depending on the nature of their intent. If you tell them you are in good health and life is wonderful they may seem surprised or ask more specific questions such as whether your eczema has become any worse recently. Sometimes they may not ask you directly, but enquire through a friend or family member. If they feel that they are not having the desired effect then the intensity or nature of the attacks may be increased. If you are in this situation it is important to continue your cleansing and protection and to be vigilant for any changes in your energy field. It is also essential that you keep up the impression that all is well and that you are not allowing them to affect you even if they are, because after a while they will invariably give up. Remember that your intention and determination needs to at least match theirs if not better it. An affirmation, either repeated verbally or mentally at least once a day might be "I only allow positive energy to enter my energy field." You might also imagine yourself inside a ball with mirrors on the outside to reflect away anything sent to you. On the inside of your mirror ball you could choose to put more mirrors which will keep magnifying all the Light surrounding you.

A very effective method to stop an attack is to write the name of your supposed attacker on a piece of paper and to freeze it in an ice cube. This is done with the intention of stopping the attack and not harming the person as after all you do not wish to attack them. You may even have the wrong assailant. In that case this method will not harm or affect them in any way. If you have named the correct person then the attacks will stop all the time the ice cube remains frozen. Beware of power cuts to your freezer or of someone using your ice cube in their gin and tonic!

A curse may involve thought forms, symbols or payment to a third party as previously described. Some curses are specific and are directed to one aspect such as your business, money, relationships or health while others are global and affect every aspect of your life. Some are family curses and may have originated several generations before. Again these may be specific or general and they might just affect for example, the male members or one line of a family. In these cases, using the previously described ball   analogy you may be completely unaware that you are holding the ball at all. Once you become aware of this then you have to decide what you wish to do with the ball. You can continue to carry it around with you maybe throwing it to other family members from time to time or even passing it onto your children. On the other hand you can decide to let go of the ball and contain it somewhere safe or even destroy it.

In the treatment of a curse it is often sensible to find out the nature of the curse and who placed it. My preferred method is to tune into this person and ask to see the original scenario. This can be done if the curse was made in this lifetime or several hundred years ago and assists with the healing process. If you know why the curse was made and what the originator intended then you can carry out any necessary reparation, perhaps asking for understanding or forgiveness on behalf of your ancestors. This in itself may be sufficient to remove the curse. If a ritual was used or a symbol then as described before, the ritual can be undone and the symbol drawn backwards to erase it. You may also wish to say something appropriate such as "I release any negativity related to this curse and I ask for forgiveness and healing for all affected." In cases of family curses I always send healing back down the ancestral line as well as to the person who made the curse.

Conclusion

In life it is always more beneficial to think positively. We have all heard the maxims "like attracts like" or "as we reap so shall we sow" or "what you give out you receive back tenfold." If you are thinking and acting positively, apart from feeling better about yourself and the world around you, then you are more likely to attract and manifest positive energy. You will recognize those days when you get up feeling irritable or a bit down and the world appears to be a much more difficult place to be and you feel things are against you.

Much of my work is encouraging people to be strong in their intention and positive in their thinking. Positive thoughts provide energy and strength. Negative thoughts disempower and drain us. When you catch yourself thinking a negative thought immediately turn it around and try to make it positive. A very simple example is that you wake up and find it raining. You could feel miserable or you might think how beneficial the rain is for the garden. If you feel as if you are under psychic attack, rather than thinking how dreadful your life is or how bad your attacker is, you might think "I do not accept any negative energy from any source. I radiate and attract positive energy. I am strong and protected."

We are all responsible for our thoughts, emotions, behavior and the healing of our old wounds caused by past experiences. What we think and feel is what we manifest. If we continue to maintain our angry, jealous, fearful, selfish, negative thoughts, feelings and experiences we manifest anger, jealousy, fear, selfishness and negativity. If each individual on the planet worked to think positively and connect with the energy of love, joy, peace and compassion then we would manifest positivity. What each of us manifests affects other people, animals, plants, the Earth and the Universe and impacts on what in turn is created. If we want to be calm, centered, energetically strong, healthy and in balance then we can achieve that state by changing our thoughts, feelings and behavior.

The more you think positively the easier it becomes. The more positive your energy field the stronger and healthier it is. This means that not only are you physically healthier, but that you are also more protected. The more Light or positive energy you work with the higher the vibration and the faster the frequency of your energy field. As this happens the more you are protected from darker, negative, denser energy that vibrates at a lower and slower frequency. The nature of any psychic attack means that the energy used is dark, negative and heavy. Once you understand this then any form of negativity is easier to work with. Just as light extinguishes the darkness, positivity overcomes negativity.

On one occasion a man who was fully aware of the nature of my work very interestingly decided to attack me by sending all sorts of images, symbols, thought forms and entities to me. I saw these various attacks over a period of about four days come towards me usually quite rapidly, but all of them stopped at the edge of my energy field and could get no further. They were therefore unable to do me any harm and were easily dismissed. After four days of this continuing I sat and tuned in to see who was sending the attacks and saw the man in question. Having asked for guidance I then pictured him clearly in front of me and without emotion said to him telepathically "I give back all that is yours." Instantly I saw everything that he had sent to me including images that I had forgotten, fly back to him. Suffice to say he has not attacked me again.

CHAPTER FIVE
VARIETIES OF ENTITY

The word entity as explained earlier means something that has a distinct existence. This term therefore applies to us as living, incarnate beings as well as to the discarnate beings ranging from Angels to demons. In this chapter I will alphabetically outline the different types of entities that you may come across on your journey through this lifetime. Techniques for the actual removal of any negative entities will be covered in chapter 8.

Aliens or Extraterrestrials

As the word "alien" tends to be a derogatory term I use extraterrestrial or ET to denote a being not of this planet. I have never assumed that we are the only life forms living on one of the many planets in the Universe. It makes sense to me that in the vast cosmos there are other forms of life as well as here on planet Earth. Some of these may be more intelligent than us, some less. Several years ago however, I did not believe that extraterrestrials might be attached to humans. Then I met one. Since then I have met a number of ET's from different dimensions who have attached themselves to people for various reasons.

Some individuals are aware that they are guided in a positive way by an ET rather than by the usual Angel or Guide. Many of these people become aware that not all of their other lives have been on Earth. In past life regression clients sometimes discover that this has been the case for them too. In this life we have incarnated as human, in other lives we may have been an alternative form of being.

In a few instances I have found ET's that have apparently run from their own planet to hide within a human energy field, perhaps being pursued for having done something they shouldn't in their own dimension. Some of them appear to be quite young. Most often the ET's are attached in order to gather information and experience what it is to be human. Their energy is commonly a very mental one and there is little or no emotion. They can be communicated with quite easily telepathically. I have found that even when communicating with entities from different cultures that language is not usually a problem. My telepathic conversations are always in English.

Often the client will notice a metal taste in their mouth which indicates the presence of an ET in their energy field or one attached to them by an apparently metal attachment or implant. If you have a metallic taste in your mouth please do not jump to the conclusion that you have an ET with you! A taste of metal can also of course, be caused by amalgam fillings or other physiological reasons.

ET's are usually easily dealt with by quoting Universal Law which says that they may not negatively affect any other being. They are very aware of this and will often obey an instruction to withdraw. Any attachment or implant also has to be removed. In the case where removal of an ET is difficult or an escort is required, it is possible to summon a senior being from the relevant planet or dimension to come and remove their colleague.

Angels

Angels are servants of the Light, aspects of the Divine that have never incarnated. They are spiritual entities that usually have to be summoned, but occasionally come uninvited. There are different levels and types of Angels. The Archangels are perhaps the most commonly known and called upon, the main four being Michael, Raphael, Uriel and Gabriel. There are many other Angels that represent various qualities or energies. You do not need to know who to call upon. The call will be heard and responded to by the most appropriate Being. Angels do not attach themselves to a person's energy field with a negative effect. So if you have a spirit telling you it is an Angel, but having an unwanted effect upon you then it is most likely a Shape Shifter.

There are a number of Angels that can be summoned to assist in spirit release work and these will be identified in chapter 9. There are also Dark Angels which work on the lower astral levels with the spirits trapped there. They frequently appear in a dark hooded cloak which hides their Light. When a spirit on the lower levels is ready to progress it will often be escorted to higher levels by a Dark Angel who may then reveal its Light.

Animals

Some people have the spirit of an animal attached to their energy field. This is frequently a pet of which they were particularly fond. I have mostly found dogs, sometimes cats and on one occasion a horse. A common animal energy I have found with people is that of the wolf. This animal is a teacher and a very loyal and protective energy to have with you.

Many individuals especially shamans work with Power Animals, but just as with a Guide they are not normally attached in the energy field.

Ascended Masters

The Ascended Masters are the great healers, teachers or prophets who previously lived on the Earth and are now in spirit. They are from all cultures, religions and civilizations. The Ascended Masters include legendary figures such as Jesus, Mother Mary, Buddha and Krishna as well as saints, gods, goddesses, devas and deities. You may call upon any Ascended Master to assist or guide you and each has specific issues, goals, aspects or qualities that may help. A number of the Ascended Masters are helpful in situations of spirit release including Kuan Ti, Melchizedek, Sanat Kumara and Merlin.

An Ascended Master will come when called, but will not attach to you.

Demons

My personal experience with demons is that they differ in shapes, sizes and levels of intelligence - just as humans do. Demons are often referred to as Dark Force Entities or DFE's. Demons come singularly or in groups. The demon may be attached to other earth-bound spirits that are also with the client. Some demons are at the level of a thought form as described in an earlier chapter. These will be very limited in their communication and will often just repeat the intention with which they have been programmed, for instance to destroy the victim. This communication may be made telepathically with the therapist or the client or it may use the voice of the client to speak aloud. Thought form demons may be dissolved or returned to their creator.

The next level of demon is very similar in nature to a thought form as demonstrated by its limited ability to communicate. It may well have a number of phrases and threats which it will repeat. Some demons will use growls and grunts instead of words, usually intended to intimidate. Frequently demons will admit to having a discarnate master who is outside of the body or energy field of the person. Others will become extremely abusive and any therapist/healer cannot afford to be easily offended. It is wise to assure the client that they are not to be shocked or feel ashamed by anything the entity does or says through them. I stress that I am aware that it is not them, but the demon that is reacting in this way.

At the other end of the demonic spectrum is the demon that is extremely dark and dangerous. This type of demon often acts as a master to many others. It will frequently not condescend to talk to you and will consider itself to be very powerful and fully in control. It may attempt to convulse or physically throw the client around the couch or room, or to assault the therapist. If it does speak it will often attack the weakest and most vulnerable aspects of the healer. It will try to provoke you into fear or anger – if it   succeeds it has won and it will know it. If this happens you will probably not be able to remove the demon and will need to refer the client to another therapist. To deal with this type of demonic entity you require complete fortitude, a total lack of fear, a very high level of self-knowledge and an inability to be shocked or offended. This type of demon is intelligent and does not generally become confused or doubtful. It will usually demonstrate contempt and hatred for humans. The demon frequently requires a forcible removal from the client which may prove to be extremely difficult. This needs to be carried out by a competent and experienced spirit release practitioner.

Elementals

People often become confused about elemental spirits. Elemental spirits are those of the earth, air, water and fire. They exist in nature and in their pure form are very positive and essential. In terms of spirit release we refer to attachments of elementals or nature spirits in more negative terms. I refer here to the elementals that have been contaminated through human negativity. I have found spirits such as gnomes, elves, bogarts and sprites in houses, not all of which are causing problems. The situation may just require some negotiation to allow all parties to co-exist peacefully. Some elementals in houses however, have fun by causing mischief to the occupants. These can be dealt with in a similar way to the low level demonic entities, almost on the level of a naughty child in some cases. They should be dealt with firmly and with compassion.

I have also found various elementals attached to people which identify themselves with natural phenomena such as stone or trees. They will quite readily with assistance return to their natural environment. The important thing to remember here is that not all entities are released to the Light. If they are elemental or nature spirits they are usually returned to the Earth. This is why I ask for all entities to be taken to an appropriate place. I do not therefore need to make that decision myself as my spiritual helpers will take care of it.

Fragments

A fragment is a part of us, an aspect of ourselves that becomes detached from the whole usually through a trauma of some kind.

These may be seen psychically attached by a fine cord to the person's body. I will often find one or more fragments attached to people who have experienced severe abuse. During the abuse the fragment detaches from the consciousness and the body. When seen psychically the fragment will appear to be the age of the person when the abuse took place. This aspect of the Self loses its ability to grow if it is detached from the whole being. It will often retain a memory of the abuse and most certainly the feelings such as fear and pain. In other cases people may fragment due to traumas such as an accident, surgery, losing a loved one or even moving house.

Sometimes fragments can simply be re-attached by revisiting the place of the accident or the beloved house that was left behind. More often the fragment is returned through a soul retrieval process which includes communicating with the fragment and the client to find out why it left and what it needs. Often a great deal of reassurance is required and the now adult client has to agree to take care of the much younger aspect of the Self that left. Both need to be reminded that the danger has now passed, the time is different and they need each other in order to be whole. The fragment is given healing and then brought back, usually through the Heart chakra, but it may be replaced anywhere into the body. A shamanic practitioner will usually facilitate this process through drumming and breathe the fragment back into the heart or head. A healer might carry this out through visualization. The client may be fully involved in the process.

Ghosts

Ghosts are spirits seen in houses or in any other place. There are two basic types of ghost. The first is a spirit that is active, conscious and may be communicated with. It may or may not be earthbound. The second has no consciousness and is purely an imprint, residue or memory of a situation or emotion. (See Imprints). Both types may be seen as shadowy figures or even as solid three dimensional people that seem quite real until they disappear or walk through a wall. Ghosts might be experienced as a drop in room temperature, a physical sense of touch or perhaps with goose bumps or tingling. A ghost will often appear at certain times or in specific conditions. This might be a time of day or year, or when the atmospheric pressure or weather is of a particular type and might indicate an anniversary of some kind.

Many ghosts can be communicated with and the reason for their haunting established. Once the reason is understood and resolved the ghost may be released. One earthbound spirit/ghost I talked with had been throwing the current tenant out of her bed on a regular basis. She had moved into the lounge and had been sleeping on her couch for some time. When I asked what the problem was he explained that in his previous occupation of the flat he had hidden money under the bedroom floor. He was aware he had died in hospital and had returned to collect his money! A simple resolution to this problem was to ask what he was now going to do with the money. The penny dropped (excuse the pun!) as he realized that of course he wouldn't be able to do anything with the money and he went into the Light very swiftly.

Some people are happy to live with a friendly ghost for many years. Not everyone is sensitive to the presence of spirits and so not all occupants or visitors to the house will even realize a ghost is there. Working to clear houses of negative energies, ghosts, geopathic stress and so on will not be covered in this book.

Guides

A Guide is an entity which is a servant of the Light, an aspect of the Divine. It is a wise spiritual being that was once incarnate and brings guidance to humans with the aim of helping us in our development and progress on this plane. Guides may be summoned or more usually will appear of their own volition. Every person has at least one Guide; a personal Guide which enters and leaves this incarnation with them. Many people work with more than one Guide during their lifetime according to their needs. Guides have different skills and aspects just as we do. Whereas the personal Guide may multi-task, others may be a wise teacher, healer or protector, help to create music or poetry or assist in business ventures.

Some Guides are with us constantly. Others will come and go according to what is required at the time. So when I am giving healing my Healing Guides arrive. When I am giving a psychic reading my Committee of Seven arrives. A Guide does not attach itself into your energy field. It will never take control and affect your thoughts, emotions or behavior in a negative way. Even sensitives who work through overshadowing or in full trance with a Guide are working with agreement and respect for each others energy. The sensitive allows the Guide to come in and take over their physical body and voice in order to communicate. At the end of the trance session the Guide leaves and the sensitive returns to full awareness without harm.

If a Guide tries to attach itself to your energy field and instructs you to carry out tasks with which you are uncomfortable it is probably a Shape Shifter. In chapter 9 we will be looking at safe methods of connecting with a genuine Guide.

Helpers

A helper defines any positive entity that may arrive to assist. This might be an Angel or a Guide or it might be an ancestor, another discarnate human or a power animal. For example, my grandmother who died before I was born has always visited me since I was a young child. For a couple of years a woman dressed in the St. John's Ambulance uniform tended to arrive when I was teaching. Her job when she was alive was to travel the UK teaching first aid so she brought her skills to assist me.

Humans – Living

Frequently I clairvoyantly see the two dimensional form of someone such as a living parent or ex-partner in a client's aura. This indicates that not only are they corded to each other, but they are closely energetically linked. This is not healthy for either party as it can drain energy at the very least. In addition there may also be an unwanted transmission of feelings or thoughts between the two people. Separation is essential to allow their individuality and freedom. The process used is very similar to a de-cording with the addition of containing the attached person in Light and moving them out of the client's energy field.

A psychic vampire or someone carrying out a psychic attack, as described in earlier chapters, may also be seen in the auric field of the victim.

Humans – Deceased

The most common attachment is an earthbound human spirit clairvoyantly seen as three dimensional. There are many reasons why some deceased people remain earthbound and this will be discussed later. An earthbound spirit can usually be easily identified because they often retain their ailments and disabilities. They do not just visit, but stay around and might cause problems such as noise or movement in the house or interfere with electrical equipment such as televisions or clocks. They may attach into the auric field of a loved one or a stranger who is energetically open to them. Some spirits wander in this way for many hundreds of years attaching to different people as they go. The reasons for their attachment to certain individuals are varied and will be discussed later.

In death our physical body dies, but our spirit does not. This is why the dying process is often referred to more accurately as "passing into spirit" and the deceased as "in spirit." In normal circumstances as our spirit body or consciousness leaves the physical body we pass into the Light. We are usually met by loved ones or by Beings of Light who help us on our way. I must stress that for the majority of people this is the case when they die. They go into the Light very easily and happily, losing any ailment, pain or disability as they do so. In my experience the deceased person's spirit is often around for a few days after their death and attends their own funeral. Many people believe that the spirit then undergoes healing and an evaluation of their life before moving on into the next stage of their development.

After physical death of the corporeal form many spirits may not be contactable through a medium for the first few weeks or months after passing as they are undergoing their own process. This is particularly the case if someone was very sick when they died. In this instance although the physical body recovers quickly as it enters the Light the psyche often retains the memory of distress and pain. The spirit body therefore needs to be given a great deal of healing when the person passes. After this time a medium may be able to contact them to provide you with proof of their survival and comfort in your grief. The spirit of your loved one may also visit to see how you are doing, to give you a sense of comfort or even to pass on some helpful information. Their visits to this dimension are often brief and they will leave each time.

Imprints

An imprint is a type of ghost which does not have a consciousness and cannot therefore be communicated with, but constantly repeats the same behavior. It is like watching a video that plays the same actions over and over again on a loop. An imprint may also be an emotional feeling or atmosphere that sits in a certain place. It has literally imprinted itself into the walls or the ground and can be sensed by people who visit. A very good example of this is the Dachau Concentration Camp Memorial in Germany which I visited in 1985. It is a large site mostly empty now apart from a museum, one of the barracks and the crematorium. The energy there is still and silent, the birds do not sing and there is a deep sense of sadness.

Incubus

The incubus is a male spirit that has sexual intercourse with females usually while they are asleep. It is rarely attached, but will visit. Many people have had a single experience of this in their adolescence. Some people see the incubus in their dream, others sense and feel it. This experience may be considered pleasurable by some. (See also Succubus.)

There are also earthbound human spirits who have sex with living people. This may be a known spirit such as an ex-partner. It might be an opportunistic earthbound spirit who continues to want sex and finds a prey. Sometimes a sex abuser finds their previous victim and continues the abuse.

Parasites

In effect all attaching or possessing entities are parasitic. They need our energy to survive and therefore feed from us. In most cases the client will feel tired all the time or experience complete exhaustion without apparent cause. Some will become physically unwell as their immune system is affected and the body becomes weakened.

There are however, entities that are pure parasites. These have no consciousness or ability to communicate, but appear as a dark blob in the person's energy field. The longer they are there the larger they become. They literally expand as they feed. The bigger they become the more effect they will have on the person. If this happens the individual may feel exhausted, completely blocked and unmotivated. Fortunately they are quite simple to release as they do not argue or put up a fight. They are usually attached to part of the body or a chakra by a tail or cord which needs to be disconnected before they are dispatched.

People from Past Lives

It is quite common for a spirit that has been with you in a previous lifetime to be with you in this life as an attachment or even a possession. Occasionally they have entered while you were in the womb. Sometimes they have found you and attached during child or adulthood. The vast majority of these spirits from the past feel aggrieved in some way and hold the intention of harming the person to whom they are attached. A few past life spirits however, have found their host through a deep love and are wanting to protect and be with them. Once it is explained that they are inadvertently causing their loved one harm they will agree to their release.

In rare cases the attached person from a past life is actually a facet of you. Instead of just being able to retrieve the memories of a previous lifetime, an aspect of yourself in that life is still attached to you. Careful work is essential here as this aspect may need to be released as an entity or even integrated as a fragment or sub-personality into the whole.

Poltergeist

Poltergeist is a German word meaning "noisy spirit." There are various theories about poltergeists. It may be a spirit who is angry or wanting to create mischief. It may be a spirit who is using the psychic energy produced by a living person. The most common theory is that poltergeists are related to an adolescent living in the house. During adolescence due to hormonal and emotional changes a high level of psychic energy can be produced. The adolescent either unwittingly causes the effects blamed on poltergeist activity or feeds a genuine spirit through this energy.

We are all able to produce a high degree of psychic energy through a charged emotional state particularly involving anger, frustration or even jealousy. It may also be produced through traumatic experiences or during release of tension. This psychic energy for instance, can blow light bulbs, cause computers to crash and electrical equipment to start or stop working. It may also cause objects to move. This is not a poltergeist as such although it may produce poltergeist-like activity.

It is clear that a poltergeist spirit uses psychic energy, but in my experience this energy can be produced by adults as well as children and adolescents. I have also found some poltergeists who were actually angry or disgruntled human spirits or even elementals which moved objects and caused noise to make their presence felt. A poltergeist is able to move even large objects sometimes with surprising force and speed and in defiance of the laws of gravity. They may also make various noises around the house and even sounds that are inexplicable. This spirit is not always seen psychically, but its presence may be felt. A poltergeist basically wants attention and can carry out harmful or playful activities depending on its intention.

Shape Shifters

A Shape Shifter is able to change shape to prevent discovery of its real identity. There are living people and shamans who use shape-shifting in a positive way. However, most spirit Shape Shifters are negative.

They may present themselves as a Guide to an unsuspecting person who then allows the spirit to guide and advise them. Typical examples of this are "Guides" who present as wise old men, beautiful young women or as children. Sometimes they will appear surrounded in Light and so it is assumed that they are a Being of

Light. Over time the true identity of the discarnate energy becomes apparent as the "Guide" starts to impress the individual to do, say or think things the person is unhappy with. The "Guide" might make threats and become abusive, picking on the host's weaknesses and doubts. No true Guide would ever do this. The person realizing their mistake then has problems disconnecting from this Shape Shifter. In chapter 9 I will describe how to check that you are working with a Being of Light and not a masquerading spirit.

Some entities use the astral shell or envelope of a human spirit in which to mask themselves. The astral shell is the substance of the astral body which is discarded after use. So an accomplished and conscious astral traveler may use an astral shell during his/her travels and will destroy it after use. When the physical body dies and the spirit body leaves, the shell remains on the astral level for a period until it disintegrates. If the deceased held strong negative or materialistic thoughts and emotions it is thought that it takes longer for the astral shell to dissipate. A wandering spirit may use this discarded shell in order to appear as something different.

An example of this may be seen in the case of a psychic client whose husband had died a few months before. He had gone into the Light as expected and had since visited a couple of times to let her know that he was well and happy. One day the client came home and saw her husband walking down the stairs toward her looking disheveled and distressed. As soon as he disappeared she telephoned me. I tuned in and found that this was a Shape Shifter who had picked up her husband's discarded astral shell. I asked spiritually for the Shape Shifter to be dealt with, the astral shell destroyed and was able to assure the client that her husband was still fine.

Succubus

The succubus is the opposite of the incubus. (See Incubus). This female spirit has sexual intercourse with males while they sleep. Some people consider this to be a pleasurable experience.

There are also earthbound human spirits who carry out sexual activity with adults and sometimes children. This is usually a very unpleasant experience akin to rape. In one man's case with whom I worked, he was having regular sex day and night with a female spirit formerly a sex worker. He had become addicted to this and did not want to let the spirit go even though he had lost his job and his friends as a result.

Vampires

The vampire is a name given to a spirit who visits at night to suck energy from their victim. This is usually experienced as a creeping sensation from the feet up over the body and ending with weight on the chest and a sense of being paralyzed. The victim is usually unable to move or cry out during the attack. Occasionally there is sexual activity at the same time. Some people lie terrified until the vampire leaves while others fall asleep waking after the vampire has gone. Many people have this experience just once in their lifetime while a number face this on a few occasions.

In some instances, this type of night time attack is caused by a living psychic vampire who consciously visits to steal energy as described in chapter 2.

Walk-Ins

A Walk-In is different to a possession in that it is a complete and permanent take over of the person's mind and body. The theory about Walk-Ins is that an agreement is made between the two spirits. The first person incarnates in the usual fashion as a baby. The second spirit agrees to take over whenever the first has had enough and literally walks out. The Walk-In is experienced as a completely different personality and character with different tastes, needs and lifestyle. Often the Walk-In will not recognize family members or friends or remember large parts of their childhood. They may hold different beliefs and change jobs to work in completely different employment. I have never to my knowledge met a Walk-In and so cannot vouch for this being the case.

CHAPTER 6
WHY & HOW SPIRITS ATTACH

How Does a Spirit Attach?

The reasons why spirits want to attach to an incarnate person or why an individual may attract a spirit are many and varied. The "how" of spirit attachment is more straightforward to explain. Our aura is basically a magnetic energy field. As we know magnets can both repel and attract according to their charge. We all recognize people who might be described as having a "magnetic" personality and who tend to draw people to them. On the other hand there are those who tend to hold people at bay and do not readily connect with others. The same can happen energetically with spirits and so some people naturally attract them into their energy field. The individuals who are prone to this type of spirit attachment are not however, necessarily those who are also attractive to other people. So do not assume that if you are a friendly and charismatic person that you are therefore more susceptible to spirit attachment.

The likelihood of spirit attachment also depends on the strength of your auric field. If your aura is strong, healthy and complete then it is more likely to repel unwanted spirits. This does not necessarily mean that you also keep people at bay. You may well have plenty of friends and a thriving social life. If on the other hand your energy field is weak, incomplete, an irregular shape, frail in places or even has holes or tears in it then it is much easier for a spirit to enter. The aura can be weakened or even damaged by physical or mental illness, surgery, certain medication – particularly chemotherapy and anti-psychotics, undue stress, internal or external negativity, alcohol, recreational drugs, cigarette smoke and pollution to name but a few. Someone who is ungrounded or even out of their body will generally have a weakened or damaged aura. It is also true that a spirit entering the auric field may cause a hole or tear as it arrives.

Many spirits are attracted to the Light that we all have around our physical bodies. Some people project more Light than others particularly those who are sensitives, healers or regularly meditate or follow a spiritual practice. This is due to the fact that the more we work on our spiritual development, our chakras and our energy field the higher our vibration and the more we are able to open and expand our auric field. The higher our vibration and the clearer our energy the more Light we can bring in and therefore channel or project. If your energy is filled with Light it will be vibrating at a slightly faster and higher frequency than that of an earthbound spirit. This will make any attachment to you very difficult. If the spirit does succeed in entering your Light filled aura, it won't generally like that vibration and will promptly leave if able to do so.

Some spirits react to Light like moths do. You will have seen moths buzzing around a light source whether it be an electric light or a candle flame. The moth tries to get as close to the light as it can until often it burns itself or dies. In butchers shops you may have seen the electric ultraviolet fly killers which operate in much the same way. The fly is attracted to the blue light and flies as close as possible until it is zapped and dies.

If your energy field is strong and protected a spirit will not be able to enter and attach, but will be zapped just like a moth or fly. Your energy field will not "kill" the spirit as after all that would be an impossibility! It will however, deter the spirit from attaching to you. In some cases electric shock has been used in spirit release therapy as spirits do not like it and will leave the host. Some therapists, rather than use electric current, will use a loud noise such a clap of hands at the client's head in order to shock and detach the spirit.

Once the spirit is in your aura then it might attach to the physical body, an organ or a chakra via a cord. This is an easy way for the spirit to receive energy from you which is why many people with a spirit attachment often feel very drained. Sometimes the magnetic field of your aura will hold the spirit in place once it has entered. Even if the spirit then wants to leave it might be unable to do so of its own accord. The presence of one spirit may attract others to join so you could end up with a group. It is generally much easier to remove a spirit which has only recently attached than one that has been there for many years. Sometimes a normal cleansing and grounding exercise will suffice. Sometimes you might need to obtain assistance from a healer or spirit release therapist. Techniques to assist in grounding, cleansing, repairing, strengthening and protecting your auric field will be given in chapter 10.

Chakra Gateways
Gateways or portals are basically astral openings between the different dimensions. They are most commonly found in houses or

places and allow spirits to pass in and out. Gateways are also used in psychic attack to enter and leave a room or to spy on the victim. Some gateways act as exits, some as entries and others operate in both directions. Only earthbound or negative spirits would use a gateway or a portal. Guides, Angels and Ascended Masters do not require them.

A number of years ago a client came to me because she was constantly having spirits attach to her. We worked to remove them and then protected her each time she was cleared. The client diligently continued her protection techniques, but still collected spirits whatever she did. At one session I was guided to look into her Solar Plexus chakra and as I did so I was surprised to realize there was a gateway right in the center of the chakra. This gateway was operating in both directions as an entry and exit. I had never considered the possibility of a portal in a chakra before. I then checked her other chakras and found that another three also had similar gateways.

The four affected chakras were all spinning in the wrong direction and were held open. Each person has an individual pattern of spin for their chakras. Many have chakras that all turn clockwise, other peoples turn anti-clockwise and some have chakras that alternate. In this latter instance the Crown might spin clockwise, the Brow center anti-clockwise, and so on down the body. Once you have established what the client's pattern is then you can discover which chakras are spinning in the wrong direction.

The key to gateways is to cleanse, close and then seal them and this is what I did. Her chakras returned immediately to their normal direction and speed of spin. When we closed and protected each they remained secure. Afterwards the client had far more control over her energy field and stopped collecting unwanted spirits.

To have a gateway in one chakra is quite rare, but to have one in four chakras is extraordinary. This type of gateway is caused by trauma which can include the entry of a spirit, a cord, a past life issue, psychic attack or physical injury to that area of the body. Chakra gateways usually operate as both entry and exit, but it would be feasible for the entry to be at the front of the chakra and the exit at the back or vice versa. With a chakra gateway in place you will almost certainly find it impossible to close or protect the chakra. The chakra may become distorted, continue to spin in the wrong direction or even stop turning completely regardless of what you do to balance it. You may also be negatively affected by spirits, other people's issues and be energetically unbalanced until the gateway is dealt with.

Why a Person Might Attract a Spirit

In the rest of this chapter I will be covering many everyday situations that may lead to a spirit attachment or possession. It is important to stress that for the majority of time we are perfectly safe. Many people never experience a spirit attachment or possession in their lifetime. Everyone at some point in their existence however, will experience an event that I mention in the next few pages. This might be bereavement, time in hospital, drinking alcohol, seeing a therapist, having a massage or sitting in a room full of people meditating. This does not mean that you will allow a spirit to attach to you or possess you by participating in these activities. Do not allow this book to put you off living your life to the full. If spirit attachment happens to you it happens for a reason and can be dealt with.

Often when we lose people we love it is very hard to let them go. This can happen with people who pass into spirit, but also those with whom we have had a relationship which comes to an end. I frequently see living people in client's auras, occasionally a partner or an ex, commonly a parent. This usually happens when one of the participants cannot release the other or when one has become needy or even dependant. Sometimes I find that there is a co-dependency where neither will let the other go. A living person may be psychically seen as two dimensional within the energy field of the client. A deceased person has a different quality of feeling to them and is seen clairvoyantly as three dimensional. In these situations the person on some level has allowed and perhaps wants the attachment.

It may be particularly difficult to let someone go if they have committed suicide. The people left behind often feel a range of emotions including anger or guilt and wonder if there was anything they missed or could have done to prevent the death. The person who has taken their own life sometimes regrets their actions and the distress caused, wanting to explain or make redress and so remains earthbound. It is thought by some that our belief of what occurs after death affects what happens to our spirit. Many people hold the belief that if they kill themselves they will be plunged into limbo or even into Hell. Given this scenario a spirit in this situation might consider it is better therefore to attach to a loved one instead. Following a death many people are vulnerable to attachment due to their grief and strong emotions. After funerals the common event is a gathering or wake where people may drink alcohol. This can open someone up psychically and expand their auric field giving access to the departed spirit. If in addition to this they want the attachment then it is almost inevitable.

A friend of mine gave healing to a woman whose fiancé two years previously had thrown himself off a cliff weeks before their wedding. The man was found standing in her aura, earthbound and distressed at what he had done. My friend gently told the client and explained that this was not helpful to either of them. Each of them was stuck in their distress and unable to move on with their lives. The client had been depressed and was also starting to have thoughts of suicide. She was apparently aware of his presence, but could not allow herself to let him go. After much discussion the client continued to refuse to allow her fiancé's release from her energy field. In this situation without her permission, it would have been extremely difficult to successfully detach the spirit. If he could have been energetically detached by the healer then the spirit may well have been pulled back because she was not ready to let go.

Unfortunately we do not know what happened in this very sad situation. I do hope that at some point the woman had a spirit release carried out as her risk of suicide would have been high. In a case of attachment the person might feel and sense the spirit's emotions and thoughts. Many people become depressed or anxious, feel trapped or suicidal and may not realize that these are not their own feelings or thoughts, but those of the spirit attached to them. It is only when the spirit is released that the person discovers that those emotions and ideas did not belong to them. One of the classic statements that clients make when they come for a spirit release session is "I feel as if it is not me."

Some people collect one or more spirits and then refuse to let them go because the spirits give them a role or function in their life. Occasionally this is because the living person feels a strong need to help, look after, rescue or save others. They may carry out this function with incarnate people as well as discarnate. One psychic I met stated that she collected the spirits of children and animals to look after them because they were not safe anywhere else. It is very misguided to believe that we humans can care for spirits more successfully than if they are released into the Light where they belong.

I met another who spent a very lonely existence and found that if she went to certain places she would gather the spirits of elderly people. She would collect about four or five spirits and then go for spirit release to one of her many therapists. Unfortunately this lady would experience all the various physical ailments of her elderly attachments. She would recognize the release of each spirit by announcing "oh that's better I can see again" or "he's gone and taken his arthritis with him." I only worked with her for a short time as my explanations of how bad this was for her fell on deaf ears. I encouraged her to find other more suitable and probably financially cheaper activities to fill her time. Any work we did on protection and grounding was ignored and she happily continued to collect people. In the end I told her I was not going to collude with her in this dangerous activity and that I would only work with her again once she was ready to stop doing it. I therefore removed myself from her circle of therapists and have not seen her since.

On occasions I have been referred cases where one or more people blame another for passing spirits onto them. Hypothetically Amanda accuses Brenda of having spirits attached and claims that those entities are jumping from Brenda to Amanda and causing her difficulties. In this scenario Brenda may or may not actually have spirits attached. The key to this situation is for Amanda to examine why she is allowing herself to be affected rather than blaming her friend. Unfortunately it might be Amanda who has unresolved issues which are causing the problems which instead of being dealt with are projected onto Brenda. In this instance spirit attachment is only one possibility that needs to be investigated.

Some people have other life contracts, debts or issues that lead to a spirit attachment. There may be a sense of guilt or of failure, perhaps of being unable to protect a loved one, prevent harm or even death in a previous or sometimes current lifetime. If a spirit is looking for someone to take care of or protect them then this person is ideal. I have met a number of clients who have declared that they love the attached spirit and find it very distressing to consider letting it go. We tend to attract spirits to us that resonate with our emotions, thoughts, needs or issues in some way. If an individual desperately wants to love or look after someone else, but cannot fulfill that need normally then they may attract and retain a spirit with whom they feel they can do so. Sometimes this can lead to an active relationship where the person converses and in extreme situations may develop a sexual life with the spirit. On a couple of occasions I have met clients who declare they have undergone a marriage ceremony with one of their attached spirits. In one such case the woman wore a wedding ring to indicate their union.

Other people attract spirits to them with their negative thoughts, emotions or behavior. If a spirit is very angry then it will be attracted to a living person who also holds a lot of anger. The spirit will feel very at home in that angry energy field and may even increase the person's rage. The same scenario may happen with those who have a lot of greed, envy, hatred or jealousy. People who are insensitive to others, aggressive or selfish, need revenge when anyone upsets them or has an obsessive need for power and control may attract a spirit that also has these same desires and ways.

A few healers and frequently those led into the field of spirit release therapy have just one personal experience of a spirit attachment. This provides a lesson for the healer that can help them in their future work. It also proves to the unbeliever that spirits do indeed attach themselves to humans and can affect us in various ways. This usually one-off experience may also be enough to show the healer that there is nothing to be afraid of. If they then find a case of spirit attachment in a client they will have some understanding of what the client might be experiencing and perhaps how to help.

I am regularly asked by people who have experienced an attachment why they had to go through that and why their Guide did not prevent it from happening. My usual answer is that before they came into this incarnation maybe they chose this experience or the Guides allowed it to happen knowing that the person needed to learn this particular lesson. Nothing happens without a reason. In my view there is no such thing as coincidence – there is however, synchronicity. This word means "the simultaneous occurrence of events which appear significantly related."[9] It is often these synchronicities which show us our next task or give us necessary information. For instance we may ask for guidance on a particular issue and then read something in a book or hear a song lyric that gives us the answer we need. This is not pure coincidence – these signs are happening for a reason. It is up to us to recognize those signs, listen to them and if we choose, act upon them. The experience of a spirit attachment probably indicates that the person requires that learning for them to progress or develop. It may highlight unresolved issues or traumas which need to be explored such as negative emotions or thoughts, childhood sexual abuse or the need for effective cleansing and protection techniques. The event may also awaken previous powers or skills that the person held in another lifetime, perhaps as a shaman or a healer, which could be utilized in this life.

At the other end of the scale some people deliberately seek contact with spirits. Trained mediums and psychics know how to do this safely and use their skills in positive ways to receive guidance or bring comfort to a grieving family member. Unfortunately other individuals love the glamour and drama of declaring they have a spirit attachment. Some people dabble in unsafe occult practices and use such equipment as the Ouija board. I have met many people who, usually in adolescence, played with an Ouija board as a bit of fun with their friends. These individuals complain that since that time they have been plagued by bad luck, depression, anger, unhappiness or a feeling of being out of control. Some hear voices or see things nearby which frighten them. The problem with this type of activity is that there is often no control over what type of spirit makes contact with those using the Ouija board.

This can also apply to people who use automatic writing, trance, channeling or healing without knowing exactly what it is that they are doing. If you carry out unsafe activities without the relevant professional training then you may be putting yourself at risk of attracting a lower energy than you intended. On the other hand if you know how to ground and protect your energy, raising your vibration to the highest possible level before you enter a trance state or channel healing, psychic energy or automatic writing then you are quite safe. Training helps you to manage your energy properly and to recognize entities that are beneficial to work with and those that are not. Later chapters will cover more of this ground and give techniques to practice.

As we have seen in chapter 4 there are those who practice the dark arts which includes the summoning of spirits to attack and harm other people. These occultists want power and are in danger of having very dark spirits attach to them. There are also those who ask for attachment or even possession by a spirit in order to give them what they feel they lack in normal ways. Some believe they can obtain power, control or psychic abilities in this way. I know of people who have used dark energies in order to make another unwell or even in an attempt to kill them. Fortunately the people who have admitted this to me have seen the error of their ways and have returned to the path of Light before they have caused irreversible harm. I am aware that there are others who have not yet arrived at this point and continue down the dangerous path of Darkness.

We are also susceptible to spirit attachment through serious wounds or trauma. This can be physical, emotional or mental trauma and might include unconsciousness during which time a spirit may enter the energy field. The trauma could cause fragmentation, covered elsewhere, which can also allow spirit attachment. If surgery is required this provides another opportunity for a nearby spirit to connect. Under anesthetic the consciousness or the astral body separates from the physical form while remaining attached on a cord. During the time after the operation while the anesthetic wears off the consciousness returns to the physical body. However, during an operation something is generally either removed or added to the physical body and therefore a change occurs. On returning the astral consciousness does not quite recognize the body because a change has taken place and therefore takes a little while to completely re-attach itself. This accounts for some of the feelings of disorientation and of not feeling quite one's self after surgery. During the time that the astral body is separated and not yet fully connected there is the potential for fragmentation or for a passing spirit, of which there are many in a hospital, to attach itself. It is also known that blood transfusions and organ transplant can also bring the spirit or aspects of the person or people that have acted as donors to the recipient.

In a similar vein unsafe astral travel may also lead to fragmentation or spirit attachment. Even though the astral body separates from the physical body as above there is rarely a problem in reconnecting the two because a change has not taken place as in surgery. However, unsafe travel on the astral plane can lead to psychic attack by another traveler or during the absence from the physical body. It may also provide an opportunity for attachment by a spirit to either the astral or physical bodies. Once again this would be due to the astral traveler's poor management of their energy. If they have not ensured they are grounded and protected before consciously traveling or before sleep, when many people travel unawares, then they may be at risk.

Generally speaking a continued lack of grounding, cleansing, self awareness, closure of the energy system and protection may lead to psychic attack or spirit attachment. I cannot stress enough that a healthy body, mind and spirit generally equates to a strong energy field which is highly effective against unwanted intrusion. It is important for us all to recognize when we are feeling a bit low, unwell, stressed, or lacking in self-esteem and confidence so that we can deal with it. We can at the very least keep our energy as clear as possible, obtain some healing, counseling or other appropriate support while remaining grounded and protected.

Other reasons why someone might attract a spirit include being too open and unprotected with people or in certain places. Therapists sometimes leave themselves open to attachments from their clients. These might include teachers, counselors and psychotherapists, body and energy workers such as masseurs and reflexologists, sensitives and healers. If you consider what happens during a session of this nature, the therapist or sensitive naturally opens and expands their energy to connect with yours. There is an interaction on at least one level and the connection made may be mental, physical, emotional and/or spiritual. It is every practitioner's responsibility to clear and prepare their work space and themselves before seeing a client. It is also their responsibility to keep both themselves and the client safe during the session and to cleanse their energy and that of the room after each person. This lessens the risk of picking up any unwanted energy.

There are certain jobs that hold a higher risk due to the nature of the role. For example, police and fire officers, paramedics, doctors, nurses and morticians all work with people who may be ill, suicidal, dying or deceased. These are all conditions where there may be the involvement of an earthbound spirit. Any entity attaching or possessing the body will want to free itself once the energy field of that person is so weakened that they can no longer feed it. If the body dies then the entity needs to attach to someone else who can sustain it. The spirit will choose the person on the scene to whom they are attracted. We will be looking in the next section at the reasons for a spirit to choose a host.

In addition to people there are also certain places where there is a higher incidence of spirits than others and a higher probability of attachment due to the nature of the activities carried out in those places. For example, hospitals are very common places to pick up an attachment as people are often very sick or traumatized and therefore more vulnerable. People who die in hospital sometimes pass while unconscious or in shock and may not be expecting to die or are not ready to do so. Places such as cemeteries, churches and funerals are often frequented by spirits who are lost and confused or not ready to depart because they wish to stay with their loved ones.

Other sites where a spirit may attach are places where alcohol is drunk in quantity. Alcohol naturally expands and may also weaken the energy field; it opens us up psychically. Discarnate spirits in pubs and clubs literally wait for the effect of the alcohol to take effect and then jump on board. Other places where we might be vulnerable are therapy rooms. During many "hands on" therapies spirits may be dislodged from one client and passed to another or to the therapist. Haunted houses and offices may also harbor a spirit or two that decide to leave with you at the end of your visit or days work.

Some objects hold a spirit which may then pass to a person.

This method is sometimes employed in intentional psychic attack where an object is used to trap a spirit and then given to the victim as a gift. The spirit might stay trapped within the object and affect everyone within its vicinity or may be able to transfer from there to the victim. In some houses I have been asked to clear I have found such objects, usually ornaments of some kind or even pictures. Most of these items can be cleared in a similar way to clearing a spirit from a person.

Why a Spirit May be Attracted to a Person

Some of the answers in this section lie in the material given during the first part of the chapter. When people die they may find it really hard to let go of their earthly life and the people they love just as we may find it difficult to let go of them. There are often unresolved issues. Perhaps something was left unsaid or the person died after an argument that was never settled. I have communicated with earthbound spirits who were unhappy because they had not written a will and made their wishes known. Some want to look after the people or property they have left behind. Many life partners make promises to each other such as "I will never leave you" or "I will always look after you/protect you" and so on. These promises can bind spirits to people or places after their death.

I recently released a lady who had lived in a house she and her husband had designed in the 1930's. On her death bed she had sworn she would never leave "her" house. I used a technique I discovered some years ago where I reminded her of the house as it was in her day and re-created it with her. Using her memories and my clairvoyance which meant I could see what she was imagining,

I reunited her with her house, husband and her favorite time of year. As we know, energy follows thought and so together we had created a thought form. When this woman connected with her house and husband she was still going into the Light, but by using a different method. Sometimes it is more acceptable to the earthbound spirit for them to go to a place which holds happy memories and where they feel comfortable than to the Light in which they might not believe or in this case did not appear to offer her what she wanted. She has now left the current householders to live in peace.

I have met some spirits who were just not ready to expire and insisted on going home after their physical body died in a hospital bed. I have also met a few who felt they were not properly mourned or disposed of. One man's body had not been buried in consecrated ground and another man felt his funeral was not "fitting." A few spirits feel attached to their physical body or to an object that they cannot bear to leave behind.

If death was sudden, traumatic or violent then the deceased may feel angry, shocked, distressed or guilty. These feelings can bind the spirit to the earth not allowing them to let go. I have met several spirits who were desperate to seek revenge for their death. I have also spoken with others who were unable to say goodbye to their loved ones or ask forgiveness for a supposed misdemeanor before they passed. I released one earthbound woman who insisted she had killed her baby. In conversation with her I discovered that the baby had died a few hundred years ago when infant mortality was high, through an infection obtained during bottle feeding. She had obviously not intended to harm the child, but her guilt had held her to wander the astral plane.

Often it is the spirit's original belief system which binds them to the earth plane. For example, I speak with many who believe in Hell and that when released from the person to whom they are attached they will be thrown into the fires of damnation and be in terrible pain for eternity. Others believe they have done such terrible things in their life that they need to be punished. They sometimes think that the Light will not accept them or that their loved ones also in spirit, will not want to know or forgive them. Others simply do not believe in life after death. When they subsequently find themselves living after their physical body has died they become confused and desperately hold on to their original beliefs.

If someone dies in hospital while anesthetized, drugged or comatose then they may not realize that the physical body has died and can become confused or afraid. This misunderstanding is a very common one and can happen to anyone who dies in almost any circumstance. I have had to explain to many spirits that their physical body has died and they are continuing to live in their spirit body. I also have to explain that this is why people have not spoken to them or acknowledged their presence because they cannot generally be seen or heard. These spirits are easily released into the Light once they understand.

On one occasion I went to clear a house and met a female spirit who had been seen by neighbors looking out of an upstairs window. She was unaware of her death, but did realize that she was in a strange house. Her daily pattern while alive was to wait looking out of the window for her husband to return from work. He was frequently late and she suspected he was having an affair. As the woman did not remember her death I took her back to that time to facilitate her understanding. She had died in hospital during an operation under general anesthetic. The hospital was on an energy line that passed through the house where she now found herself. Her spirit had traveled via that energy line from the hospital to this unknown house. Feeling very confused the woman had resorted to her old behavior of waiting at the window for her husband to return home even though he never came. Once I had explained the situation to her she was very relieved to see her parents coming to meet her and left with them. And yes she was right, her husband had been having an affair, but I didn't need to tell her that.

Touching on a very emotive subject now, a very common type of spirit that I see with women is that of an aborted, miscarried or stillborn child. If you are a woman who has experienced this or a man whose baby has been lost in this way please do not panic and assume that your baby's spirit remains earthbound. I generally find that this only happens when the spirit of the child has not been acknowledged or mourned, or does not understand why it has not lived. I have frequently facilitated conversations between women and the spirits of their babies in order that each achieves understanding and resolution. I then ask for someone in spirit to come and collect the baby and it is commonly the child's grandmother, great grandmother or another family member who arrives.

One fascinating case I worked with was a woman who presented with lower abdominal problems without medical cause and an inability to gain weight. When I tuned into her I was immediately guided to focus on her womb. Inside I could psychically see the spirit of a very angry small boy. On talking with him I discovered that he had not understood why he could not be born and was extremely angry that his mother had ended his life. The client confirmed she had terminated a pregnancy twenty years previously. Since that event she had miscarried a few times. She now had an adolescent son with behavioral problems who appeared to be very angry and was unable to live with his mother as he professed to hate her. The pregnancy and birth of her son had been fraught with difficulties.

I explained to her that there was a spirit of the baby she had terminated still residing in her womb. I asked her to talk to him about that time and explain why she had made the decision to abort him. After a while he seemed to understand, she asked for his forgiveness and immediately I felt her womb start to contract. It was with great surprise that the two of us realized she was going to give birth. Having never done this before I did wonder if we needed hot water and towels! Within a few minutes she felt something coming down the birth canal and the spirit baby was delivered. I then handed him over to a very beautiful woman in spirit whom I have since come to recognize, as she often arrives to collect children.

My understanding of this situation was that in the surgical abortion of the fetus the etheric part was left behind in the womb. Every time the woman became pregnant this etheric part would cause a miscarriage. The intention being that if she did not want him why should he allow another baby to live in "his" uterus? The son that she did give birth to had probably spent his time in the womb in conflict with the spirit which might explain why he was so angry and full of hate and why the pregnancy was so difficult. It is also possible that on his birth, part of the etheric of his brother may have attached itself to him thereby causing an angry and difficult child who didn't like his mother. After the clearance the woman's health changed for the better. She asked me to see the son to clear him as well, but he never came for an appointment.

This raises the discussion continuing in some quarters that during surgical procedures involving abortion or organ transplant a healer should be in the operating theatre. Each cell holds the memory of the whole and therefore a spirit or the memory may be trapped within. There are many cases of organ transplant where the recipient of the donor organ starts to have memories that are not theirs or cravings for certain food and drink that they did not have prior to the operation. There are other cases where the recipient's behavior changes and certain personality traits of the donor appear. Rather than have to release the spirits afterwards a healer in situ could do the work with both the donor organ and the recipient's physical body to cleanse and prepare both for the surgical procedure. There would probably be far less organ rejection as the body would more readily accept the cleansed organ as its own. In regard to abortions the healer could ensure that the spirit of the fetus understood what was happening and was released safely.

I have also seen the spirits of children who have died young around their parents. Usually these are simply visiting and may appear the age they were when they died. Very occasionally the parents have been unable to let go of the child who has then remained earthbound. Once these children are released they tend to grow up in spirit to the age they would have been if they had lived. Sporadically I have found children that have been sacrificed in another lifetime and are attached to their killer as a reminder of their actions. Often these adults will report a sense that they have done something terrible or express feelings of guilt without a known cause.

I have also met spirits who have attached to a living person with the intention of helping them. This can happen to children and adults who are in distress, scared, lonely, depressed and very ill or who have been in an accident and ended up in hospital. The spirit wants to take care of them and may have been a natural rescuer in life. There are of course spirits who do not wish to help the living person, but instead have negative intentions. Like attracts like and as we have seen in the previous section a spirit may be attracted to a living person who holds a lot of fear, anger, guilt, despair, jealousy, resentment, depression or addictions. If a spirit is angry it feels at home in the angry energy field of an incarnate person. The spirit feeds like a parasite from the angry feelings and also from the person's physical energy. Many people with a spirit attachment feel tired or even completely drained most of the time.

If the spirit has been addicted in life to drugs, alcohol, sex, shopping, cigarettes or food for example, then this can continue after death even if they are aware of their passing. In order to feed their craving the spirit may attach to someone with a similar addiction. Sometimes the attachment may be made to someone who does not crave alcohol, but starts to do so once the spirit attaches. Many chronic drinkers have a number of spirits with them which may be seen psychically in their energy field. The drinker will often be heard talking to their "demons" and may have lost their home and relationships while feeding the needs of the spirits. Some alcoholics do not appear to get drunk and this is literally because the attached spirits drink the alcohol. The alcoholic often has to increase their intake in order to get an effect from their drink.

Some spirits attach because they recognize and want to harm the host. It is said that sex abusers on their death will sometimes attach to their victims in order to continue the abuse. I have spoken with many entities who have tracked down their victim sometimes over several centuries in order to wreak revenge. They have been attracted to the spirit energy of the person and often fail to recognize that this spirit now inhabits a different body in another time and has no conscious awareness of the events that took place several centuries earlier. These revenge-driven entities can do enormous harm to the physical body causing illness, disability and sometimes death.

I have also found spirits who have tracked and attached to the host who they claim is a close sibling or partner. They are often quite difficult to dissuade from their attachment even though they might come to accept that the incarnate person no longer remembers them. I sometimes have to resort to "if you truly love them then you will want the best for them and let them go." This usually tests whether the spirit is telling the truth or not. If indeed they do feel a strong bond and love for the person then they will accept they are inadvertently harming them and allow the release. If this is a trick or a lie they will disclose their true intent and are dealt with in another way. Unfortunately not all spirits suddenly become truthful in death!

Sometimes a contract has been made in another lifetime and the spirit arrives to continue that contractual arrangement. This frequently involves non human or dark entities who announce that they are working for a master, not least the Devil in his many guises, and that it is time for payback. Dealing with contracts will be covered in more detail in chapter 8. There are also the spirits that have been sent by a living person in the nature of a psychic attack as covered previously. These latter will often acknowledge the attacker as their master and agree to return to them.

The last type of attachment which I will cover here is the extraterrestrial. While working with clients I have found a number of these attached. The ET's are obviously different to the human, non human or dark spirits as they are still very much alive. Their usual reason for the attachment is to collect information and to experience something of what it is to be human. Some however, have attached in order to hide or to steal energy. Quoting Universal Law often does the trick and they will withdraw.

In the next chapter we will look at the signs and symptoms of spirit attachment and possession and the differences between these two phenomena.

CHAPTER 7
SPIRIT ATTACHMENT AND POSSESSION: SIGNS AND SYMPTOMS

Spirit Attachment or Possession?

The difference between spirit attachment and possession is simple. Spirit attachment occasionally referred to by some as "obsession" is where the entity has attached itself within someone's aura or energy field. Possession is where the spirit has actually entered the physical body. So let's look at this in a little more detail.

If the spirit is somewhere in the auric field it may be seen clairvoyantly and can also be sensed or felt. A healer will often discover an attached spirit in this way. The entity might be felt as a heavy, tingly, sharp, dense, static or cold patch and there may well be a hole in the aura. There might be an emotional energy such as sadness or anger or it could even feel threatening. The spirit would possibly be seen as a dark or grey shape or even as a figure with full details of clothing and appearance. There may be an unpleasant odor or a scent of tobacco or perfume that does not belong to the client, but comes and goes. Physical symptoms can be experienced in the area where the entity is attached. So if it is on the left hand side there may be problems down that side of the body such as aches and pains or various injuries and weaknesses. If the spirit is attached to a chakra then that energy center will most likely be out of balance and need clearing. If attached to an organ, similarly there may well be problems with that part of the body.

A spirit may also cause such phenomena as a bad taste in the mouth, popping in the ears or even tinnitus. The clients might feel they are physically touched and some report being pushed, hit, tripped up or burned on various parts of their bodies. Others notice their body or the bed in which they are lying feels as if it is vibrating. In one case an attached spirit could be heard snoring while it slept!

If you have an entity attached then it can affect the reactions of those around you. This is because we all unconsciously and intuitively react to energy. In this way we can take an instant like or dislike to someone we meet for the first time without any rational reason. So even if another person cannot see the spirit you have with you they might react to it. If that spirit is angry, brooding and threatening then others might treat you with aggression or fear because they feel threatened and defensive. I have worked with many clients who related stories of being shouted at or even physically attacked for no reason, sometimes over many years. They have often been completely bewildered by this and cannot understand what it is they have done to warrant this behavior from others. Once the spirit is removed other people will frequently react quite differently. Obviously there is a psychological issue here as someone who has experienced ill- treatment and abuse for years for whatever reasons may have learned to accept this as normal behavior. It may take a long while for them to trust and feel safe and confident with people.

In cases of spirit attachment to a client there is only a small chance that the healer or therapist will be affected by the entity. It is possible that during a treatment specifically intended to remove the spirit it will try to attack the healer in some way. However, if the healer is unaware of the presence of the spirit or not attempting to release it and is just giving a normal healing s/he is usually quite safe. It is not common for the entity to transfer in these circumstances particularly if the healer is properly grounded, cleansed, attuned and protected. There are instances of transfer of spirits from the aura of one person to another and this may be for any of the reasons given in the previous chapter. It may also be a case of being in the wrong place at the wrong time. Remember, once a spirit is in a human magnetic field it can be quite difficult for that entity to extricate itself unaided. This fact can prove useful when talking to a spirit that considers itself to be in control and have all the power. To point out that it is trapped and cannot leave without help somewhat deflates it.

It is possible to find any number of energies within an aura and with experience the healer/therapist will be able to differentiate between them. For example, there may be one or more spirits of different types, thought forms created by the client themselves or sent by someone else, the energy of a living person and cords to people or objects. A few people have a whole myriad of energies within their aura that require clearing, but most clients in this situation have just one or two. There are of course clients who have strong, clear, healthy energy fields with none of the above and this should not be forgotten! Not all spirits trapped within an aura are aware that their physical body is deceased whereas others will have that understanding. Not all will be intending harm to the person to whom they are attached, but a number will. Some have previously known the client while others are strangers. A few realize they are stuck and want help and therefore make themselves more noticeable. Information on all of these phenomena is covered throughout this book.

Entities are often very clever and may well have tried to prevent the healing appointment taking place. In cases of both spirit attachment and possession I have had instances of the client's phone call being disconnected or with such bad interference that a conversation has been impossible. Some people have been made physically immobile on the day of the appointment so they cannot attend. Others have had a car crash or various bizarre events have happened on the way to me.

True possession is a different phenomenon to spirit attachment and is actually not as common as often assumed. Clients contact me and say they are possessed when it is really a problem of spirit attachment. They will also say that they have an attachment when they are actually under psychic attack or vice versa. It is imperative for a spirit release therapist to carry out an assessment and reach their own diagnosis. It is particularly important to be able to do this if the person arrives saying they have one of these problems when in fact they don't. The healer/therapist has to be confident enough to inform the client if there is nothing present and not collude with false beliefs. This applies even if another healer or psychic has referred a client to you saying that they require the clearing of a spirit and you find they don't. It is essential to be both tactful and truthful in these situations. I have seen clients who had been informed they had a spirit with them which could be cleared by that same individual for a large sum of money. This is possibly a misunderstanding (or at very worse a con) and either they do have an entity which can be cleared quite simply or there is actually nothing there. In these situations I am not generally tactful! The lesson here is to seek a healer or therapist through recommendation or a reputable source.

Possession is the presence of one or more spirits within the physical body. Consequently the spirits cannot be clairvoyantly seen or sensed within the aura of the person. The type of entity that possesses can vary. If it is human it will be deceased and in my experience is never a living person. It will probably be very well aware that its corporeal body has died and will often be intent on harm or at the very least have little consideration for its host. I have also found elementals and various types of dark and non-human spirits living within a human, including extraterrestrials.

Thought forms can also exist inside the body and this internal type is usually sent by another as a psychic attack. The thought form may be placed within an organ or an area of the body. I have treated clients with various thought forms placed for example, in their bladder which caused painful or restricted urination, in the uterus to prevent pregnancy and in the intestines to cause pain, general debility and weight loss. A thought form in situ may also be activated by the attacker through telepathy. So the victim may feel physical movement or receive thoughts and images from their attacker. These types of thought forms are not possession, but psychic attack.

The interesting thing I find with a true possession is that the spirit within sees someone like me and usually cannot resist showing itself. It commonly does this once the client sits in the chair opposite me and we start to talk about why they think they have a spirit with them. The usual way an entity will expose itself is via the eyes. As I sit talking with the client their eyes will change. In most cultures when talking with people we tend to make eye contact with one another. The eyes are said to be the window of the soul and show our true nature. We can often gauge from someone's eyes how they are feeling and what type of person they are. When the eyes change as the spirit shows itself you realize that you are looking at someone or something completely different. Something that has a completely different mood and personality and may indeed be quite menacing or merely observing you. The eyes often change shape, size or color and will stare directly at you. The face of the person may change in part or completely. This might be brief, but it is enough for you to realize that there is a possession in place.

The person is often unaware that something else is looking out of their eyes or their face has altered. It is not helpful or professional to show fear or abhorrence when these changes take place. I have seen this happen a number of times over the years and always look straight back at the entity showing it that I am not intimidated. The one time I found it briefly unsettling was sitting with an older woman when, while she was talking, just one eye changed and looked at me. So there I was looking at her one gentle, kindly blue eye and the entity's larger, menacing, black eye for a couple of minutes. One very useful question I learned to ask when I noticed this type of phenomenon is "when you look in the mirror what do you see?" In every single case I have found that the client has also seen something else looking back at them even if they have only seen a glimpse of it. Often I am the first person they have admitted this to and only in response to my question.

It should be noted however, that an occupying entity does not always wish to be seen. The classic example of this is when the affected child or adult suddenly becomes angry or their mood changes. It is at these times that the afflicted person refuses to look at anyone. This might be because the entity doesn't wish to be seen in an "out of control" moment or simply doesn't want to be discovered.

On only one occasion in many years have I seen long term, physical changes due to a possession. A man came to see me with pain in his right shoulder and numbness on the right side of his face. This client had been told by a psychic that he had "something" with him. He had quite grey hair, a bit of a tummy and what appeared to have been a broken nose although he denied ever breaking it. When I tuned into him I immediately saw and felt a short, portly, pompous man who had a liking for women, red wine and sweet food. Immediately after removing the spirit the pain in the client's shoulder and the numbness in his face disappeared. Within two days he found he had a lot more energy and motivation. After two weeks the client phoned to report that his tastes for wine and sweet foods were disappearing, his hair had returned to dark, his nose no longer looked as if it had been broken and his tummy had reduced.

The *only* way a possessing spirit can transfer to another host is through physical contact. Once it is in the physical body it cannot escape without help. The entity usually isn't aware of this fact until informed this is the case. If you are working as a healer or sensitive and realize that your client is possessed then, and I cannot stress this strongly enough, *do not touch them*. In this way you are perfectly safe. The client needs to be referred to a competent and experienced spirit release therapist to be freed from the entity.

If on the other hand you are fully aware of the possession and totally confident in your ability and competence to deal with it safely then you may work with physical contact in order to remove it. In this instance what you may feel as you make contact with the client's body is a vibration that is not theirs. I have also seen the entity moving around under the skin or through the abdomen of the client as they lie on a couch. Many entities will move around the body as you try to release them because they mistakenly think that somehow they can evade you. The individual might feel a lump in their abdomen, throat or chest as this happens. Occasionally the limbs will move or the body will writhe. In rare instances the entity may attempt to hit, punch or even strangle the client and occasionally the therapist. Sometimes marks appear on the body as you work or the client has reported large, inexplicable scratches on waking in the morning. In a couple of cases I have felt a second heart beat. If the client is not pregnant then you know there is a problem! The spirit of course does not have a beating heart, but it may try to shock you in this way.

If a possessing spirit does decide to transfer you will most likely feel a rush of energy from the point of contact. So if for example, you have your hand on their shoulder then you will feel something like electricity run up your arm. Some healers have experienced this when they have made physical contact with a person to whom they are giving healing. Usually the spirit which enters a healer finds that it doesn't like their Light filled energy and so will withdraw or run down through the healer's body, out through the feet and back to the client. This happens quite fast and it is important for the healer to disconnect from the client, check that the spirit has completely left them and to clear any residual energy from themselves immediately. They might then continue the healing by working off the body or choose to end the session and refer the client onto a more experienced practitioner.

An entity of this type tends not to like the energy of a healer or anyone whose life force has a high vibration. Spirits generally exist on the astral and sub-astral planes and therefore their energy vibrates at a slower, lower frequency. The energy of higher spirits such as Guides, Angels and Ascended Masters vibrates at a high, fast frequency. People who work as healers and sensitives generally spend a great deal of time in their training and daily practice on their own energy management. We work to bring in more and more Light and to cleanse and expand our aura so that we can channel more energy through us. As we do so our subtle bodies become lighter and finer and vibrate at a faster, higher frequency. If a spirit actually manages to enter this high frequency energy field full of Light it will not feel very comfortable and will want to leave immediately. Anyone, not just healers and sensitives, can work through meditation and a regular spiritual practice to improve the vibration and clarity of their auric field. Achievement of this means you are at significantly lower risk of spirit attachment or possession. Techniques for cleansing and raising the vibration of your subtle bodies are given in chapter 10.

There are times in which I have deliberately taken a spirit into my body or energy field in order to release it although it is not my preferred way of working. I will cover this topic in chapter 8 on treatment. The essential issue here is that I know how to release the entity immediately if I do this. I have treated a number of clients who are themselves working as complementary therapists or health professionals and who have very helpfully removed a spirit from their patient and then become stuck with it. This is not a safe practice and the rescuer can easily become the victim.

Symptoms

So let us look now at the symptoms that someone might experience if they have a spirit attachment or a possession. Many of these symptoms can also be attributed to other causes so if you read something that applies to you do not immediately assume that you have a spirit on board. Generally a person with an entity attached would have a range of symptoms and not just one or two. It is also the case that some people with a spirit attachment are completely unaware of its existence.

The most common symptom is to feel drained or exhausted for the majority of time without physiological cause. This is because the spirits feed like parasites on physical energy. The immune system might also be adversely affected and therefore provide less resistance to infections, coughs and colds. Over time motivation or enthusiasm may also reduce and so the person fails to achieve their aims in life. A useful question to ask the client is whether the symptoms came on suddenly or gradually. A sudden onset is quite common – as the spirit arrives it brings the symptoms with it. The sudden arrival of pain or nausea, an addiction, ailment or illness might indicate where the entity has attached and may be a condition it had when alive. Pain in the back is common as many spirits arrive from behind. Some non-human parasitic entities insert a tail down through the victim's spine in order to attach securely. The posterior of the aura in many people tends to be more vulnerable because they are less aware of it. The energy field at the back is therefore less protected, perhaps weaker and contracted closer to the body.

Many spirits attach quietly and so the onset of symptoms is reported to be gradual. The entity bides its time becoming well enmeshed in the energy field before making itself known. Many spirits bring symptoms to a particular organ and so might affect eyesight, hearing, the digestion or the heart, for example. Sometimes the medical profession is unable to find any pathological problem that explains the symptoms.

One very interesting case of distant healing involved a man who was becoming more unwell as time went on. He had lost a lot of weight, was exhausted and most of the time confined to the house. We had spoken over the phone and I confirmed that there was indeed a male spirit in the house which in fact the client had seen on more than one occasion. The spirit had started to become attached to him at times and was certainly draining his energy. We agreed a time that I would do the work. A couple of days later the client phoned me to say he had been to see a nutritionist. Unexpectedly she had informed him that he had a tapeworm and asked him to return within a week for the treatment. Once I had carried out the distant healing work and released the male spirit the client returned to the nutritionist who carried out the test once again. This time she was surprised to find that there was no evidence of a tapeworm. It would appear therefore, that the client was exhibiting the symptoms of a tapeworm belonging to the spirit I had released.

There is a distinct possibility that someone experiencing Body Dysmorphic Disorder (BDD) has a spirit attached. In this condition the individual will have a distorted perception of their body image. This might be a part of their body for example, their ears, nose, teeth or hair in which they perceive a flaw and become obsessed with this imperfection. The client may desire surgery to correct this defect which to others is quite simply minimal or even non-existent. BDD also includes eating disorders such as anorexia and bulimia where the person views themselves as grossly overweight while others may see them as severely underweight. In a case of spirit attachment it may be the views and beliefs of the spirit that are being expressed and which distort the client's own perceptions.

One woman was referred to me having seen her doctor regarding depression which did not fit the usual pattern, but came and went suddenly. When I tuned into her I immediately put my hand on her lower back because that was where the spirit was attached. In answer to my question as to whether there were back problems I was told she had undergone various tests for lower back pain. The tests had shown no pathological cause and her X-rays were fine. Her doctor diagnosed her with osteoarthritis of the lower back being unable to come to any other conclusion. Once the spirit was released the depression never returned and neither did the back pain.

Some entities cause food cravings – chocolate and meat are apparently common. One man used to get up at 3am every night to eat chocolate. Once we had removed the spirit he continued to do this because over the twenty years the entity had been there his body had learned this behavior. All his other symptoms however, vanished. This is an interesting point to consider. Sometimes we do not know which symptoms the spirit brings and which are our own. This can lead to the mistaken belief that normal bodily symptoms produced by other more natural causes are due to entities. One man insisted his stomach noises and rumblings were spirit related even though they coincided with his having eaten or drunk something or when he was hungry. Noisy stomachs are normal for many people including me! The other issue it raises is that if a spirit has been in residence for a long period of time the person has probably adapted to it in some degree. This can include changes in behavior, thinking, sleeping patterns and food likes or dislikes. If someone is left with a pattern they do not like they then have the task of working on changing that once the entity has gone. Often people with a spirit attachment have become used to thinking in a negative way because they are used to facing constant difficulties. After the release they have to work very hard at thinking positively and changing their outlook, attitude and behavior.

A number of spirits crave the alcohol, nicotine or drugs to which they were addicted in life. This can cause the host to start drinking, smoking or using drugs which of course, can further weaken their energy field and lead to multiple spirit attachment as well as other social problems. There are cases of people who have imbibed for periods of a few months and then suddenly stopped. A few months later they suddenly start drinking again and are unable to understand why this happens as it does not coincide with any particular event. I often hear "It doesn't feel like it is me that is drinking. I have no control." In my view people do not normally *suddenly* start or stop using sometimes significant quantities of alcohol or drugs for no reason. Generally there is an increase into the habit and then a decrease of use before quitting with some decision making and determination being integral to the process.

As I have stated earlier, once attached a spirit generally cannot leave the aura without help, but there are some exceptions to the rule. I have known some that were able to come and go, some that started out being attached to a site such as a house and then connected to a person or vice versa. Others are more apparent at certain times such as night time so the person is spirit-free during the day. In the case of intermittent use of alcohol or drugs it might be the case that the discarnate spirit arrives and stays for a period and then leaves again. This might explain the erratic start and cessation of the problem.

A spirit attachment or possession can also include sexual activity. I have known clients who suddenly became very sexually active without feeling that they had any control over who they had sex with or the nature of the sexual activity. This can be very distressing if you find yourself engaged in unwanted activity or with someone with whom you would not normally consider being intimate. Several clients have reported being raped or their genitals and other body parts being touched by a spirit. These distressing events would normally be reported to the authorities, but how do you report a spiritual rape? In some cases these spirits are sent as a form of psychic attack. I have also known of cases where living people have used astral travel or projection in order to have sex with someone against their will.

Many people with entities attached to them will be affected by the emotions, thoughts and perceptions of those spirits. The person may feel angry, sad or guilty for example, without knowing why they are feeling like that. Feelings of depression, anxiety and panic attacks are common in cases of spirit attachment. In some cases the human host feels suicidal without understanding that it is the entity who is feeling this way. Perhaps the spirit died through suicide or is in despair over their current situation and can see no way out. It could be the case that someone with an entity attached, especially if it is constantly torturing its host may be led to attempting suicide in order to escape their tormentor. There may also be a drive to self harm through body mutilation such as cutting the skin or to be self destructive in other ways.

Often these feelings come on suddenly and without an obvious reason. This can be the same for thoughts. Thoughts and ideas come into your mind and the immediate response is "where did that come from?" Clear examples of this are when the thoughts are abhorrent to you. For example, I have worked with distressed clients who kept thinking racist, sexist or homophobic thoughts which they knew were against everything in which they themselves believed. The unpleasant thoughts depart with the entity. A gay friend of mine phoned to say he thought he had a spirit attached. When I asked why he told me that he was on the train to work that morning standing behind a young blonde woman and had sexual thoughts about her. I told him he had better come round immediately! We cleared a heterosexual man in his forties who had been there about a fortnight.

Clients will often say "this is not me" or "I don't feel as if I am in control." They complain of being taken over by a feeling such as rage without cause. There may be sudden changes of mood and uncharacteristic changes in behavior or personality. This individual may become irritable and increasingly difficult to live with. Commonly their families, partners or friends will tell me that the affected person will at times appear to become a different character. I have known people who are themselves very weak or immobile through illness or old age that will demonstrate strength normally beyond them and who perhaps need to be restrained to prevent them harming themselves or others. I worked distantly with a very elderly lady who had severely restricted mobility due to arthritis and had been unable to leave her house for a long time. She suddenly took to going out, walking long distances which should have been medically impossible, eating food that she had always hated and was no longer able to recognize family members or remember significant life events. Once she was cleared of the spirit attached to her she returned to her usual state of health, mobility, diet and memories.

There is invariably disturbed sleep and strange dreams in cases of spirit attachment. Sometimes the entity will show itself to the person in their dreams. This is different to a normal dream or nightmare as it tends to be the same figure that is seen over and over again. The figure will often suddenly appear in the dream completely out of context as if it is out of the control of your mind and just appears of its own volition. The spirit in the dream may speak to you or demonstrate that it is in control and what it wants to achieve. It may also appear just as you are drifting into or out of sleep when we are all more receptive to spiritual communication of both positive and negative kinds.

Many healers or sensitives when working in or looking at a client's energy will sense a block above the Crown chakra and another beneath the feet. Some entities particularly the more malevolent ones consciously do this as it blocks the ability to connect with the Earth and the Universe. The person will therefore have great difficulty in grounding their energy, connecting and communicating with their Guides, meditating and so on. Some lose the ability to visualize or to dream, especially if the Crown or Brow chakras are blocked. This level of disconnection over time can lead to feelings of isolation, despair and helplessness. A spiritual crisis may ensue. The individual might become very ill and weak as they lose the ability to allow Universal and Earth energy to flow through them and nourish them. It is essential to clear these blocks as quickly as possible to enable them to return to optimum health and well-being.

Some people find that the entity causes them problems with concentration or memory. They can no longer mentally focus on specific issues and decision making becomes difficult. Occasionally there are gaps in memory and considerable periods of time are lost. I am not referring here to those times we all experience when we are driving a car or doing another fairly automatic activity and do not remember the last ten minutes. I am talking about those times when you have absolutely no memory of doing or saying something, being somewhere or with someone else.

This brings me onto the subject of mental health. Some of the people I see claiming they have a spirit attachment or are possessed have a mental health issue. In many cases both are true – they have an entity attached plus they have a mental health condition. It is important for a spirit release therapist to be able to differentiate between those that need referral for a mental health assessment and those that can benefit from a spirit release procedure. Sometimes both courses of action are appropriate.

I have experience of working in the mental health field and in my view there are clearly cases of specific mental illness. There are spirit release therapists who believe however, that all people demonstrating states that might attract a diagnosis of a mental health condition have a spirit attachment problem. You have to decide what you think. It is clear that one can bring the other. For example, those that become mentally ill can then attract a spirit through the damage done to their aura by anti-psychotic medication. They may also attend a day center, be admitted to a mental health ward or become an outpatient in a mental health hospital. Even if they do not have a spirit at the start of their illness they may acquire one or two by being in these places where entities abound. Others clearly become mentally unbalanced due to the distress of having a spirit attached to them. It is also true that many more people cope with a spirit attachment without becoming mentally unwell.

The condition of Multiple Personality Disorder (MPD) or what is now called Dissociative Identity Disorder (DID) can also cause memory gaps, disturbances in personality and behavior. Dissociation produces a lack of connection in thoughts, emotions, memories, actions and/or sense of identity. The theory behind this condition is that due to severe and often repetitive trauma one or more parts of the psyche have split off into sub-personalities or alter egos in order to survive. These sub-personalities are usually the age of when the trauma occurred and may or may not be the same gender as the person. The alter egos can develop so strongly that they are able to take over completely. Each personality may have different habits, physiological aspects, skills and abilities. There are cases where one alter has a condition such as diabetes whereas the core person does not. The personalities may wear very dissimilar clothes and eat different food. There are also instances where one might be able to drive while others cannot.

This phenomenon is very different to fragmentation and the need for soul retrieval that we discussed in earlier chapters, where an aspect of the psyche is separated and frozen in the time of trauma and emotion. This fragment does not take over as a separate personality. The phenomena of spirit attachment or possession can cause this type of fragmentation as the trauma to the host may be severe. Once the spirit has been removed then the soul retrieval and integration can take place.

In conditions of MPD the important issue is to integrate the personalities if at all possible. More commonly however, the conscious cohabitation of the personalities is more achievable than total integration. Unfortunately MPD may also be an ideal situation for a spirit or two to attach without being noticed. How do you differentiate between a personality that needs to be integrated and an entity that needs to be released? This takes time and experience. A spirit will usually acknowledge having entered the client at a certain time and will be able to describe an earlier existence. A sub-personality however, will not acknowledge a life before coming into being. Many sessions would need to be spent communicating and observing the various personalities to ascertain which belong and which do not. To get it wrong and attempt to integrate the spirits while separating the real aspects of the Self would be disastrous.

Another symptom that needs to be addressed is that of someone hearing voices. In this situation any doctor who does not recognize the possibility of spirit attachment will usually diagnose the condition of schizophrenia or a psychosis. Generally people who are mentally unwell will tend to hear voices that tell them negative things or even to harm themselves or others. Commonly the voices which are a product of a mental health issue will be heard *outside* of the head. They might be said to come from the walls, radiators, TV or radio for example. It should also be noted however, that some people with a mental illness may also hear these voices inside their head.

Voices from the spiritual planes are heard *inside* the head except in rare occasions where for example, there may be a need for urgency. With Spirit Guides the words spoken and the guidance given is always helpful, caring and compassionate and often received as thoughts. Attached entities are also usually heard inside the head even if they are outside of the body in the auric field. They may say some very negative and intimidating words. The visiting spirits of loved ones who have passed will also be heard inside the head of the medium. In this instance, the spirit has usually come to offer evidence of their survival after physical death and words of comfort to the bereaved.

The ability to differentiate between a mental health condition and a spirit attachment comes with time and experience. There is a need to assess for instance, if the person appears to be in this reality and is fully coherent in their thoughts and behavior.

In the next chapter we look at various methods of treatment used to release spirits affecting living people. Usually this release ends the symptoms caused by the spirit. Occasionally some symptoms remain afterwards such as low energy, weakness, ill health or mental infirmity, but the majority goes on to make a full recovery.

CHAPTER 8
TREATING SPIRIT ATTACHMENT AND POSSESSION

Responsible Spirit Release

Having considered the types of entities attached to people and the symptoms they may cause, it is now time to investigate methods of dealing with them. In the field of spirit release there are many techniques for carrying out a clearing. I would like to remind the reader that the spectrum of spirit release is a wide one. Many people are very capable of carrying out a spirit release at the softer end of the scale. These are the cases where there are human spirits attached who do not intend any harm and may not even be conscious of where they are or how they got there. At the extreme end of the spectrum it is essential that only someone who is well-trained, experienced and fully competent should consider carrying out a spirit release. I refer here to the cases of malevolent entities intending serious harm. It is this nature of spirit release that can be highly dangerous. At all times the practitioner must be able to remain compassionate and focused in the energy of their Heart center. The practitioner must also remain strong, unwavering and assertive. My emphasis is always on helping and if necessary educating both the client and the entity. Spirit release or rescue is not merely about banishing an entity in order to aid the client.

Some practitioners work with colleagues while some work alone. I prefer to work alone or should I say without other incarnate people. I do of course work with my team of spirit helpers and so technically I am never on my own. If you do choose to work with other practitioners then you need to agree a method of working and the roles that each of you will take to ensure clarity between you. You cannot afford to work in a group where there is confusion or no-one in control as the entities will make the most of this vulnerability and attack the weak links. I would suggest that if you work with even one other person you need to have a good knowledge of each other and the skills you each have so that you are co-ordinated and efficient. In a group situation it is essential that there are no egos getting in the way of the work. The focus always has to be the safe release of the entity as much as the safety of yourselves and the client for whom you have a duty of care.

However and wherever you choose to work in this field you must be able to manage your energy at all times. You must prepare yourself and the environment for the clearance. This includes strong grounding, cleansing, protection, raising your vibration, expanding your energy field, connecting with the Light, asking for assistance from your spirit helpers and for permission from the client or their representative. In distant or remote work the request for help does not always come directly from the host of the attachment, but from a parent, partner or friend. The victim may be in a mental health hospital, in a coma, of insufficient mental capacity or in any other state in which they are unable to give their informed consent for the work to take place. Informed consent means that the person with the spirit attachment fully understands their condition, the healing that will be carried out and the possible effects of that healing. In instances where there is no direct consent for whatever reason then you should always ask for permission to carry out the work from that person's Higher Self. If you receive a negative response from the Higher Self or if the person directly states that they do not want healing of any kind then you do not proceed. It is not for any of us to make a judgment as to what we consider to be right and then carry out a piece of work that may not ultimately be in that person's best interests.

An entity that has been with the client for a short time can be much easier to remove than one that has been attached for a number of years. You may find that one method does not work and so you need to use another or even refer to a different type of practitioner. Some practitioners specialize in one specific method of spirit release. The benefit of this is that they can become very proficient at that one technique. The draw back is that if they have a client on whom it does not work then they have nothing to fall back on. I use several methods and can therefore be quite flexible according to the client's needs. I still however, need to occasionally refer people to another practitioner as sometimes none of my particular techniques work with that individual. No-one can ever be one hundred percent successful.

Some people come to me aware they have a spirit attached, but not wanting to know anything about it. They want it removed quickly and without their involvement. In these cases and generally when working with children I work completely silently with the entity. As I work I talk to the client reassuringly so that they do not become afraid or worried about what is taking place. When working with children it is important to work as quickly as possible as youngsters are not usually good at remaining still for long periods. I have also carried out a clearing while the child is sitting on a parent's lap, drawing a picture or playing with a toy. It is important not to cause distress to the child or accompanying adult.

In general I have as few people present as possible during a clearing. On occasion a client asks that a friend, partner or family member remains in the room during the session. If this allows the client to be more relaxed and there are no confidentiality issues then I agree. It is important that the therapist is able to protect all those present during a clearing and is able to work unhindered. One of my greatest irritations in any healing session is the ringing or vibration of a cell/mobile phone. This invariably interrupts my concentration and therefore the safety of the session. During treatment of a psychic attack or a decording it is not uncommon for the attacker or person corded to attempt to make contact and a phone will often ring at the crucial point. I strongly suggest this matter is dealt with before the clearing begins.

There are many people who arrive for a spirit release session feeling frightened or at least very anxious about what it going to happen. It is important to remain calm and reassuring, explaining how you are going to work and what they might experience. I have taken many people through a clearing with their full involvement and understanding of whom or what they have attached to them. Not one of them has been overly frightened or upset by what they have experienced during the release and are often surprised at how "normal" it all is. At the end of the session all clients should feel relaxed, relieved or lighter in some way.

My aim during any healing session is to maintain a calm and

controlled environment. I do not perform dramatic actions or speeches during a clearing. I often talk with the client while we are working which helps to keep them relaxed. I explain what is happening, check they are feeling OK and allow them to ask questions as they wish. If I am going to remain silent for a while I will inform the person of this. I have had clients who report attending very dramatic spirit release sessions where there has been screaming, writhing, vomiting and even collapse on the part of the practitioner. In my opinion none of this is necessary and can be very frightening for the client.

It is on a very rare occasion that external disturbances will be caused by the entity. This might include the rattling of windows and radiators, the movement of plant leaves and pets might become agitated if left in the room. In a couple of cases while treating psychic attack sent by a professional, a sudden storm has produced thunder and lightening at the salient points. I find that an appropriate use of humor in these situations will disempower the dramatic effect and can also reassure the client that there is nothing to be afraid of. If as a therapist you commonly find that this type of disturbance occurs during your clearing sessions with clients then you need to look at your own energy to see why you might be causing these manifestations.

There are of course, people who come for healing completely unaware they have a spirit attached. In these cases I remove the spirit without telling them, having asked for permission from their Higher Self. At the end of the healing they may have felt something leave or a weight lift from them or just feel better than when they arrived. The client does not need to know that I have removed an entity. Indeed it may well frighten them unnecessarily. It is unusual in this instance for the client to realize what has taken place, but if they do and ask questions then of course I am honest with them. I might simply say that I removed an energy that did not belong to them. I provide more details if they specifically ask, but it is important for the client to have time to digest the information and feel they can come back to me after the session with any further questions.

The idea of having a spirit attached in your energy field can be extremely frightening for many people. On a few occasions someone has attended an appointment without saying anything about the entity in the initial discussion, but afterwards told me they realized there was something attached to them. In this instance I will give confirmation if indeed they were right. Most people generally want reassurance that the entity has now gone and may want details as to what it was and why it was attached to them. It is important that any feedback to the client is not dramatized, but given in a very normal and grounded way. If you do not make a drama out of it and speak gently and reassuringly then the person is more likely to remain calm and accepting.

A number of people have been sent to me having been told frightening things by other healers and psychics. Some were informed they had many entities with them or the spirit was described in an alarmist manner. If the person then has to wait to see me, as invariably I have a long appointment list, they remain in a state of fear and anxiety. It is often only relevant to tell the client that their energy needs to be cleared. The healer may explain that they are referring them to me because I specialize in this type of energy clearing. When healers refer to me in this way I usually carry out the clearing in one session and then suggest they return to the healer so they can continue their work together. The majority of people who see me for a spirit release only need to have one appointment. I aim to work fast and effectively and have managed to clear as many as seventy spirits in one hour. It is usually unnecessary to keep someone coming back time after time.

Many people who come to see me for spirit release have only one, two or perhaps three spirits with them. There are those however, who have groups of spirits attached and I may need to deal with them as groups or as individuals depending on the situation. When working with more than one entity I always ask for the strongest one to come forward first. This assists in various ways. For example, if an entity has identified itself as the strongest you can therefore ask it to act as the leader for a group and to take them all off into the Light at the same time. With others you might need to encourage the entity telling it how courageous it has been to step forward. It can also be the case that once the strongest entity has gone then others are more able to present themselves for release. If you do need to carry out more than one session with a client then the spirits left may be the weaker, more co-operative entities which can wait until the next session.

It should also be mentioned however, that commonly the entity which identifies itself as the strongest is also the most difficult. It is invariably this entity that is causing the most distressing symptoms to the host. In that situation the entity hopes to block its own release as well as the rescue of the weaker spirits also with the client. Very occasionally the most difficult entities are identified later in the clearing process. In this scenario the entity tends to remain quiet during the clearing in the hope it will not be discovered. The spirit assumes you will not find it and so it can continue to feed from the host's energy and cause a variety of problems. Fortunately as the clearing progresses the more intuitive therapist will uncover the hiding place and realize that an entity remains.

There are times when a particular spirit has another entity attached to it. This is commonly discovered during communication with the spirit or on encountering a problem at the point of release. The spirit might try to leave, but be held back. If a second or even more entities are attached to the first then they must be released before the original spirit can be freed.

When several entities are present with a client they might not be aware of each other and may feel isolated and alone. These will need to be released separately. In other cases however, some entities are very aware of the presence of others and may well feel frightened or intimidated by them. During a spirit release it is important to keep checking if any entities are left. Responses from the client at the beginning of a session often inform me that there is a single entity or perhaps three present. I then find that having released those there are in fact more. Entities are not all brave and will frequently hide until they are uncovered or until they feel bold enough to come forward. This is commonly the case for children in spirit who have attached themselves to the host for care and protection. I sometimes find that an entity will wait until the last moment having watched others leave until it trusts both me and the process. I have also experienced sessions where the last entity present, eventually fearing remaining undiscovered and left behind, will suddenly declare itself. In some ways it is a bit like removing layers of an onion until nothing but the client is left.

If you are unable to remove all the entities in one session it is perfectly acceptable to instruct those remaining to stay quiet until the next appointment when they too will be released. I have used this method very successfully in situations of spirit attachment to both clients and houses. The essential issue here is that if you make an appointment to assist a spirit in its release then you must keep that appointment. Otherwise the spirit can become very angry and agitated and re-commence making difficulties for the client or house owner.

All spirits should be released in a controlled manner either up into the Light, down into the Earth or taken to a holding place. Other energies such as thought forms, cords and residual energy also have to be dissolved and cleared. It is important as you work that you contain whatever energy you have removed safely. Rather than dispersing it into the room I often choose to contain it in a "psychic dustbin" by my side. At the end of each session or sometimes if it gets really full, several times during the session my Guides will empty it for me and provide another. The other essential part of the work is that whenever you remove something from someone's energy field regardless of whether it is a spirit or another type of entity you must fill the space. Whenever you remove a thought form, cord, entity or even an emotional block this will create a void in the energy field. If you leave this void it is possible for something else to establish in that place.

Responsible spirit release needs to include a healing of the aura, mending any holes, tears and splits that have been caused. Some entities are attached to the body or a chakra via a cord and this needs to be dealt with as described in chapter 3. If the spirit has used or created a gateway within the chakra system then this also needs to be cleansed, closed and sealed as previously described.

Regard should be given to the Crown chakra connection to the Light and the Base chakra connection to the Earth as these are commonly affected by the presence of an entity. This should be followed by a rebalancing, grounding and protection of the energy field. The client must be encouraged not to dwell on their experience, but to let it go and move forward with their life. If they must talk about their experience then they should be careful to use the past tense. The person should be encouraged to think and behave positively, perhaps changing any old patterns that might have been established during the attachment.

I usually suggest taking it easy for at least twenty four hours after a spirit release. Some clients experience this kind of work as akin to having surgery. Even though the process does not generally involve pain, I have removed something from them even if it was not physical matter. I strongly advise no alcohol for twenty four hours, but to drink plenty of water, eat good food and rest. Many people feel tired after a release and need to go home and sleep. I have also known a few women who have unexpectedly menstruated after a clearing, even in one case a woman who was in her menopause. This is a very natural way for the body to cleanse itself and is not a cause for concern. Some people's energy takes a few days to settle. Others feel and look lighter and energized immediately at the end of their session. I also inform the client that they may phone me with any further questions or concerns afterwards. Many people feel big differences immediately while others notice more subtle changes that occur over a period of weeks. The process of spirit release is as individual as each of us.

Techniques

So let us now explore the variety of techniques that may be used in spirit release. You might employ just one method or a combination of techniques during a session. Do draw upon your creativity and allow your clients to use theirs. Whatever method(s) you utilize you must ensure you are well trained and competent in each and also adequately insured.

Prayers/Blessings

One way of releasing a spirit from a client is to recite a prayer or a blessing and this is always included in a religious deliverance service or exorcism. This type of deliverance calls upon the power of the Divine and commands the spirit to leave. It relies upon the intention and belief of the person carrying out the release just as in any other spirit release technique. In my view, no genuine method relies totally on the beliefs of the client although it does help if that person is at least able to relax and trust the practitioner. The client is able to block or prevent the release if they are not fully ready to let the entity go. Many practitioners say a prayer or a blessing as part of their methodology before, during or after the release has taken place. Sensitivity for the beliefs of the client is paramount and I would advise prayers to a specific deity are said silently to prevent offence.

Sprays, Oils and Essences

There are a range of sprays, oils and essences which may also be used to assist in a spirit release. I use a few drops of Crystal Clear[10] in a small bottle of water to clear my own energy and that of the room before and after each client. The same company produces another essence called Astral Clear which is stronger and can be used to clear entities. The benefit of both these essences is that they have no scent and can therefore be used in any situation. A few of these drops may also be added to your bath or put into the palms of your hands and spread through your energy field. Other excellent sprays such as the Australian Bush Flower Space Clearing or the Alaskan Purification essence[11] are scented and therefore may not be acceptable to everyone. In my view, a spray on its own is not generally going to clear a spirit firmly attached in someone's aura. It will certainly assist you in keeping the environment clear and raise the vibration of the room's energy. It will therefore add to your prayer, blessing or any other method you choose.

The Alaskan Essences include one called Soul Support which is an emergency spray designed to bring strength, stability and balance during any kind of trauma. So you might decide with the client's permission to use this in their aura during or after the process. In chapter 10 on energy management there are references to other sprays and essences which might also be useful after a spirit release to restore balance and grounding, to repair, strengthen and protect the aura.

Oils such as tea tree, pine, benzoin, eucalyptus, olbas, juniper berry and clary sage may also help clear the energy of a room or person. These may be burned in an oil burner, as incense or a couple of drops placed in the palms, rubbed together and then taken through someone's aura. Certain oils should not be used during pregnancy so care must be taken in this instance.

Crystals

Some people work with crystals in healing and a few crystals are helpful in spirit release. It is said that the white crystal selenite removes entities from the aura. Amber, bloodstone, black obsidian, black tourmaline, kunzite, rose quartz, smoky quartz, amethyst and clear quartz are also good for clearing negative energy.[12] Those who use crystals in spirit release tend to use a wand or a single or double terminator crystal, which is a many sided quartz crystal with a point at one or both ends. The point is used to concentrate and direct energy and can therefore be used as a tool in releasing a trapped spirit.

Crystals should be regularly cleansed and this may be carried out using visualization, intention, smudging, candle flame, healing, dowsing or placing them on a bed of quartz crystal. If the crystal has changed or lost its color and requires deep cleansing and re-energizing then bury it in a pot of earth for about three weeks. Do not put a crystal straight into the ground because when you go back for it the crystal will no longer be there as it will have traveled. Non water soluble crystals can be washed in water and allowed to dry naturally. You might choose to dry the crystals in sun or moonlight to re-charge them. Whatever you do please do not cleanse crystals in salt which is abrasive and can harm them.

Machinery

A number of people have informed me they have released spirits using a radionics machine. One woman happily said that she could pick up the presence of an entity on her machine and then would open the window and the machine would send the spirit outside. When I asked her what she thought had happened to the spirit she had no idea. The danger with using any method without conscious intention is that the spirit may well leave, but sending it out through an open window without direction means that it will just attach to the next person it meets. This is not responsible spirit release. It merely passes the problem onto another poor unsuspecting person. In any spirit release you must always ensure that the spirit has been safely removed to an appropriate place and one from which it cannot return.

A method used by Dr Carl Wickland[13] for more than thirty years starting in the late nineteenth century, involved applying electricity to the patient in order to eject the spirit into the body of his wife while she was in trance. Through dialogue with the entity using the voice of his wife he would then release it to the spirit world. It is possible that the ECT or electric shock therapy used regularly in the past on people with mental health problems also had the same effect of ejecting spirits. Unfortunately those same spirits may well have subsequently attached themselves to another patient or even a nurse if they were not directed to a more appropriate place. Mental hospitals are known to contain high numbers of earthbound spirits.

Sound

The use of noise can also help to dislodge a spirit from a person's energy field or a home. Once again it is not a method to be used on its own as loud and sudden noise can dislodge an entity by setting up a vibration it does not like. The spirit still needs to be guided to the spirit world and not just moved somewhere else. In this way people playing loud music or beating a biscuit tin in the corners of a room may well help to stir up and clear energy. If dislodging an entity from an individual some practitioners will use singing or toning, crystal or Tibetan bowls or even clap their hands. The latter method can come as quite a shock to the client who may well be lying peacefully with their eyes shut. If you suddenly clap your hands loudly by their ear without warning they will probably jump and possibly have a heart attack! Generally it helps to release a spirit if the client remains relaxed. So do talk to your client about what will happen during a session and before making any sudden loud noise or movement.

Complementary Therapies

I understand that various bodywork practitioners have also discovered that they can release entities during a session. These include osteopaths and cranial sacral therapists as well as those who combine healing with massage techniques. The emphasis here is on a safe release without the therapist taking on the attachment.

Acupuncture

In Five Element Acupuncture the aim is to balance the mind, body and spirit. This treatment employs a concept of Inner and External Dragons which describes how an energetic block or negative energy might be considered to be a possession. A Dragons treatment can also clear residual energy, help in grounding, stop the client from hearing voices as well as removing cords and curses. The process of the Inner Dragons is carried out first and then if necessary the External Dragons. In each procedure acupuncture needles are placed at seven specific points to release the block or what might be seen as a spirit. The acupuncturist holds the intention while they work that any spirit or negative energy is released to an appropriate place.

Hypnotherapy

There are some hypnotherapists who carry out spirit release work. Hypnosis can be used in various ways. The hypnotherapist will generally facilitate the client into an altered state and then engage in direct communication with the entity. The client will verbalize what they are hearing or sensing from the spirit. In some cases the entity will take over the client's voice mechanism and talk directly to the therapist. If the client is unable or unwilling to use this direct communication method the hypnotherapist may use ideomotor responses or finger signals. This involves programming one of the client's fingers to be the "yes" finger and another to be the "no" finger. This method will be covered more extensively in a later section on ideomotor responses.

Some hypnotherapists work with a second person who acts as a scanner for the client. The scanner is hypnotized and makes an energetic connection with the client. The entities talk through the voice of the scanner or through the use of finger signals. This method can therefore be used at a distance and without the client being conscious of the work taking place. The hypnotherapist facilitates the removal of the entities through the scanner.

Not all clients are suitable or able to be hypnotized and may have to be referred to someone who is able to use a different method.

Dowsing

Eugene Maurey always carried out spirit release at a distance and by using a pendulum. His method is described fully in his book *Exorcism*[14] and his experiences are fascinating to read. For example, Maurey has encountered prisoners who have no memory of the murders and other heinous crimes their attached spirits have allegedly caused them to commit and for which they have subsequently been convicted.

I too have used a pendulum to clear both houses and people remotely. I regularly use a pendulum while working in situ to help me particularly with specific answers. It is also possible to use the pendulum to carry out the direct clearing of a client in certain instances. In all work with a pendulum it is important to obtain three directions of movement. The "energy of the pendulum" or the "neutral position" swings one way, the "yes" answer swings in another and the "no" moves in a third direction. After each yes or no answer you direct the pendulum to return to neutral for the sake of clarity. So for example, my pendulum swings back and forth to indicate the pendulum energy or the neutral position, moves anticlockwise to show me a yes and clockwise for no. All instructions or questions to a pendulum have to be very clear and concise. "Show me a yes" will elicit a clear positive answer. While "can you show me a no?" will also indicate a positive answer as of course it *can* show you a no. To obtain your negative direction you must tell it to "show me a no." You will realize that this method is limited in that it only copes with closed questions that can be answered either in the affirmative or the negative. A pendulum cannot answer an open question such as "which spirit should I release first?"

A pendulum may be used very easily to clear a room or a person's energy field, but it will not necessarily work on all types of entities. You may also find that your pendulum starts to behave oddly or even gives you inaccurate answers. If this happens it is probably being influenced by the entity and therefore the pendulum will be of no use to you in these circumstances. If your pendulum is working well for you then the question to the pendulum might be "is there any negative energy in this room?" If the pendulum indicates there is then while it is moving in its "yes" direction tell it to "clear the negative energy, turning it into positive energy and show me when it is done." The pendulum will continue to move in the yes direction and you can tell by the force of the swing and how long it takes as to the nature of the negative energy it is clearing. When it has completed the clearing the pendulum will change direction. So it might return to the energy of the pendulum or to the "no" answer. This change of direction indicates that the work is complete. The same method might be used to clear someone's energy field or chakras.

A pendulum might also be employed above the Crown chakra to clear, balance, heal, ground or protect someone. You would use the same method as above and instruct the pendulum to carry out the task you need it to undertake. When it changes direction it has completed the task.

In some instances of an entity attachment the pendulum may be utilized to gather and contain the entity. It is a bit like winding candy floss onto a stick. You use the pendulum as it swings in a circle to wind the spirit or the energy attachment onto the pendulum. Once you sense that you have gathered the entity pull the pendulum sharply away from the body of the client. The pendulum must then be cleansed – I use my hand, intention or white Light and dispose of whatever I have collected into my psychic dustbin. If something remains in the energy or body of the person continue to work with your pendulum in this way until everything is cleared.

Physical Contact

I tend to work quite physically with people if they are happy for me to do so. Once I sense where the entity is and how it is attached to the client I might then place my hand on that part of the body if appropriate or in the auric field. I wait until I sense I have made contact with the entity and then remove it with my hand. Often the entity feels as if it is moving up through the body towards my hand and I take hold of it as soon as I can. In some cases I have had to go deeper and some clients experience this as if I have my hand actually inside their body. Invariably people can feel the entity being removed as I pull it gently from them. In cases where the entity is very resistant I might have to pull it quite hard and this might involve me pulling firmly for example, down the person's arm or leg. In these instances the client can often tell me where the entity is moving to and whether they feel it is getting smaller or weaker as we work.

It is interesting that not all entities are removed in one piece. They are after all just energy. It is essential that all pieces are cleared as otherwise it may well grow again. In the same way as hermit crabs and newts can regrow a severed limb. In one case I found a young elemental being inside a client's abdomen, a favorite place for entities to reside. I generally work with people at the start of the session to relax them and ensure they are comfortable. In this instance the young one fell asleep as the client went into deep meditative state and I simply lifted it out.

With anything I remove in this way I am guided as to what to do with it. Usually it is a case of handing it up into the Universe or to a Being of Light. I frequently see very big hands come to collect an entity, taking it into the Light. This is what happened to the young elemental spirit mentioned above. Sometimes the entity is taken down into the Earth and in other cases I see it escorted through an astral doorway in the distance. Sometimes I put it into my psychic dustbin for removal.

Visualization

Many people visualize quite well and this can be very effectively utilized in spirit release. A few entities however, will effectively block the client's ability to see, imagine or dream. For those who cannot easily visualize they can be encouraged to sense and to feel instead. I might therefore start the session asking the client to scan their body for any physical feelings, emotions or dark patches that they are not happy with. Some people find this exercise easier to carry out if they imagine a mirror in front of them and then describe what they see in their mirror.

Often the person will experience a feeling of tension, pressure or discomfort in a particular part of their body. The client is asked to focus on this area and see what comes to mind as they do so. They may relate to an emotion such as anger, fear or guilt or perhaps perceive a color or an image. I then encourage them to work with that image, color or feeling by asking such questions as "what does that color mean to you" or "tell me about the image you are seeing." In many cases the client is working in this way on their personal issues. In some situations however, they may relate to an entity that is with them through this technique. The person might sense the emotion the entity is holding or relating to, how it looks or what it wants. In a few cases the clients have actually seen the spirit that is attached to them and are able to describe it in detail and speak with it. In this way we can establish why the spirit is there and what needs to be resolved in order to release it. One very common question I am asked by clients is "why did this entity choose me?" Frequently the entity will be able to provide an answer, but not always. Occasionally the client was just in the wrong place at the wrong time, but there is usually something within them that has created a connection.

I encourage any client who is involved with me in the process to find a way of releasing the entity. Sometimes this means having to look at what it is within them that is holding onto the spirit. Why are they not yet ready to let it go? Once both the entity and the client are ready for the release to take place we agree a method of doing so. This may be me lifting the spirit out and sending it to the Light. It might involve calling upon loved ones in spirit to collect the human entities. These relatives, friends or ancestors then come to meet and take them onwards. Sometimes it is a case of returning an earth spirit to the grass, earth, trees or stones. So we would both visualize this place and encourage the entity to go there. Remember here that energy follows thought so if you can encourage a spirit to remember, visualize, smell, taste and feel where they want to be then it generally works very well.

One young lady aged about eight years old was brought to me by her mother. Mum had primed me on the phone that her daughter possibly had a spirit with her. During the first part of the session I found the girl to be intelligent and psychically sensitive. As I started work I was guided to involve her in the process. I checked this a few times as I do not usually involve children in this way. However, my team was quite clear that I should go ahead. I asked her to focus into her body and tell me where it didn't feel right and she immediately told me that her abdomen felt "funny."

This was exactly where I could see the entity situated. As we talked about this I encouraged her to see what was causing this funny feeling. The child described what I was seeing and was able to identify without any fear that it should not be there. I agreed with her and asked where it would like to be and how we should go about removing it. She decided that it would like to be far away on a beach in the sun and that it should travel by plane. So with mum and I joining in we lifted the entity out and put it in a plane seated at the window. We all waved as it left in the plane and watched it fly a long way until it arrived on the beach of a very beautiful island. Once it was happily on the beach we worked together to cleanse and heal her abdomen with white Light and then fill and protect it with gold Light. As you can imagine this session was one of creativity, fun and laughter! The result was that after a few days the mother phoned me to say that her daughter was a changed child both in behavior and also in health.

With the more difficult and resistant entities it may be a case of visualizing them being placed into a box or container of some kind before release. I have sometimes used a net of white Light to contain the entity and then we make the net smaller and tighter until it is no longer mobile and can be removed. With entities that are argumentative and resort to trickery and lies they will often agree to go somewhere and then refuse to actually leave. I work with them for quite a while to negotiate and persuade until there comes a point at which I have to get tough. At that time I will offer the entity a choice, but make it very clear that it is leaving and cannot stay where it is. The choices might be to go to the Earth, to go into the Light or to be escorted to another place where the entity will be contained and alone until it chooses a different option.

The sorts of places I describe to the entity include a dark room or a metal box without windows and no way out apart from the locked door. In one instance I described a room of mirrors to a human spirit where she would sit alone and look at herself. In this case she very rapidly decided to go into the Light after all. It was then explained to me that in her lifetime she had avoided all mirrors due to a facial disfigurement. I had been completely unaware of this on a conscious level, but obviously one of my helpers knew the facts and had guided me to use that particular imagery.

I make it very clear to the entity that if they choose the option of "the other place" and some of them do, that they will stay there until they choose something different. As soon as a decision is made to come out of their room they will be escorted to an appropriate place for them where they will be given healing and looked after. I know of other practitioners who describe a dark room, sometimes with spiked walls, where the sides get closer and closer until the box is tiny. My thoughts on this are that we need to remain compassionate towards the entity. It does not need to be harmed, but it does need to be contained. To sit alone in a room with only one's own thoughts and feelings can be bad enough.

Light Beings

Before carrying out any of my work whether it is a psychic reading, a healing or a spirit release I always call upon the Beings of Light to be with me. I ask them to work with, through and around me and to protect the space, the client and myself. I do not work alone and would never consider doing so. They assist in keeping me grounded and attuned during the work and in this way I remain safe and focused on what I am doing. See also chapter 9 on working with Guides, Angels and Ascended Masters in spirit release. Suffice to say here that Spirit sorts out who needs to work with me each time. The room is often filled with many Beings of Light to assist in the process of releasing a spirit. This can include the Guides, Angels, Ascended Masters and loved ones who are there with the client as well as my own group of helpers. So it can get pretty crowded in my therapy room!

There are times in which I might call upon a particular Angel or I notice the arrival of a specific Ascended Master which indicates to me the type of entity that I am about to encounter. For example, if Melchizedek appears then I know it is going to be the heavier end of the spirit release scale. Some of the Light Beings work in groups and others work singly or in pairs. For example, I might see my group of warriors who come to remove an entity that is particularly resistant. I have also seen Dark Angels escort an entity to the dark room described above. One will remain on guard outside the locked door until the entity decides to make a different choice.

In most instances the Light Beings will work alongside me. As I watch them work the client may feel hands upon them that are not mine. At other times I will be instructed as to what action I should take. This might involve asking the client to breathe out to assist in the removal of the entity. The guidance given to me may perhaps include what type of questions to ask or the words and images to use. It is the Beings of Light which take care of all spirits that are released or rescued from people and places. It is they who ensure the spirit is taken to the most appropriate place and not allowed to return and re-attach itself to a living person. It is the Light Beings who help me to guide the lost discarnate humans to their loved ones who are already in the Light so that they may be taken care of and allowed to continue on the next part of their journey. Without the Beings of Light, the servants and representatives of the Divine, none of us could do this work successfully or safely.

Escort

On rare occasions I have been required to escort a spirit into the Light. Once this involved a very frightened man who was unable to see or understand what was happening and I was given the honor of taking him into the Light. When he was calmer and accepted the care of the Beings of Light I returned. My experience in the Light was understandably very brief. Getting there was like climbing a very long staircase, but with little effort. On later occasions I have again seen this staircase and been allowed to escort the spirit part of the way until we are met. I return as the spirit continues the journey upwards. I am always very clear when this happens that my intention is to act as escort and not to stay!

Normally when releasing a spirit I do not see a staircase, just the Light. The spirit does not usually leave directly upwards, but the Light usually slopes off at a gentle angle, almost as if they are walking forwards rather than immediately being taken upwards.

Transfer

This technique is not to be used unless you are fully trained and very experienced. It can be dangerous unless you know what you are doing. I am aware of some spirit release therapists who *always* work in this way. Some profess to have little or no control over the spirits entering them. If this is the case they tend to have regular ill health and tiredness and can become very grey in pallor if they continue in this manner for a long period. Several people have come to me for help after releasing a spirit from another person having been unable to rid themselves of the entity residing with them. As I have said earlier it is not my preferred way of working, but I have been required to use this method in a number of cases for various reasons. If you do work in this way you need to be very sure that you do not respond with fear or panic once the spirit transfers. You must remain firmly centered in your Heart energy and release the entity quickly and totally.

The act of transfer into the body often feels a bit like electricity and can be quite uncomfortable. The spirit may also transfer into your energy field rather than the body and this can feel like pressure or a change in temperature. If this is going to happen I am made aware and prepared beforehand. Uncontrolled and unexpected transfer often occurs right at the beginning of the process at the point where you touch the client. However, it might happen later and possibly take you unawares. Before working with one male client I stood away from him as usual in order to tune in and prepare myself for contact with his energy. As I did so the entity which was attached to his Sacral center decided to try to reach out and attach to me at my Sacral center. This required an immediate response from me to detach and contain it within the client's Sacral chakra so that I could deal with it properly. There is a need for vigilance and for the therapist to remain in control of the process at all times.

The key to a controlled transfer is to allow the entity into your body or aura and immediately break contact with the client. It is important to ensure that you put sufficient distance between you and simultaneously contain the entity inside yourself. This stops it from trying to get back to its original host and gives you control. Once the entity is with me I remain very still and relaxed and focus on expanding my Heart energy which tends to calm the spirit. In most cases I have then held a silent dialogue with the entity. In this way some human spirits have shown me the memories of their death and I have experienced their emotions and their thoughts.

The very first release I carried out using the method of transfer involved a Japanese Kamikaze pilot. Once he was within me I discovered that he had been rejected by his family at the age of eight years and left to fend for himself. This had made him tough, angry and uncaring about his fate. Once old enough he signed up to become a Kamikaze pilot. He was assigned to crash his plane onto the deck of an enemy ship, but crashed into the sea instead and was fished out. This meant failure and dishonor and he was sent up for a second attempt in another plane. This time through his memory of the event I rode in the plane as it fell towards the ground. The Japanese pilot was laughing hysterically all the way down until the plane burst into flames on impact. His feeling was one of despair and fear, but also a sense of madness at that moment of achieving the death for which he longed. We spoke for some time and he agreed he was ready to be released to a place where he would be loved and cared for. He felt he had no family to come for him. What was interesting was that as we asked for someone to come to take him into the Light a group of other Kamikaze pilots arrived dressed in brown just as he was. This man was pleased that they had come for him as he had assumed he would always be alone. He left me to go with them and I returned to my client to complete the process.

Whatever type of entity you contain within you needs to be released and I always ask my team of Light Beings to assist in doing this. My task is to remain calm and relaxed during this very quick process. Generally the entity is taken directly upwards through my channel and into Light. I feel the spirit leave me and then a cleansing takes place to ensure my energy is completely clear. Only after my energy is rebalanced do I return to the client.

The importance of cleansing is illustrated by the case of a student who had carried out a healing during which an entity had transferred. She had managed to release the entity safely and wanted me to check that it was completely gone from her. Without her giving me any further details I checked that indeed the entity had been released. I was able to tell her however, precisely where it had entered her and the exact route it had taken though her head and body. In doing this I was able to clairvoyantly see a track, a bit like a tunnel that a worm might make. I then worked to cleanse and repair the damage done to her energy. If the tunnel had been left it may have caused an imbalance in her energy for some time until the body naturally healed itself.

Ideomotor Responses

Ideomotor responses are movements of the body which are not consciously controlled. The use of finger signals is where two of the client's fingers are programmed to act as the "yes" and "no" indicators. The client does not need to be hypnotized in order to do this, merely in a relaxed state. This method means that only closed questions may be asked just as in dowsing. The skilful practitioner can still hold a lengthy conversation with an entity in this manner although it does help if you receive psychic guidance from your helpers. I use this technique regularly and find that because I can directly tune into the entity present I can usually ask the most relevant questions. I can therefore generally elicit the positive responses which short cuts the lengthier process of guesswork. It is also important to bear in mind that the client is fully aware of their finger responses and so this method is not suitable for someone who does not want to know what is with them or why.

On occasion I have found some clients are unable to designate a "yes" or "no" finger. This may be because they are anxious and blocking the response or because the entity is blocking them. Many clients are amazed during this process that their fingers move entirely on their own. Even if the client tries hard to make one finger move instead of the other, invariably they cannot do so. This technique may be used to release spirits, to undertake a soul retrieval or any other work that requires access to the client's unconscious mind. As the client remains fully conscious they are also able to tell me if they see images, hear voices or experience any physical sensations while we work.

Before we start I explain to the client that the finger signals enable us to communicate directly with their unconscious mind or with any entity present. In order to program the fingers, after relaxation the process is to ask the client to focus very clearly on the word "yes" until one finger feels different to the others. The client raises that finger to indicate it is the "yes" finger. The same procedure is carried out to find the "no" finger. The client is then told to focus on the fingers and as I ask questions they are to allow the finger to rise in response to the question even if they think a different answer in their head. I then ask my first question – "is there a mind, consciousness, entity, being or spirit anywhere within *(client's name)* energy field or body that is not a part of his/her true self." Usually, because I have already psychically ascertained by tuning into the client's energy field that there is an entity present, there is an immediate "yes" response. Sometimes however, there is initially a "no" response as the entity attempts to pretend it isn't there. The simple way around this is to ask the same question three times. The Universal Law of Three's means that you cannot be lied to on all three occasions. You can try this out with friends too! On a couple of occasions I asked instead as my second question if there was an entity hiding and then received a "yes" response. Once I have established contact with an entity I explain that I am not going to harm it, but I am aiming to help resolve the situation.

In a later section I will explain some of the various dialogues which may take place with entities during a spirit release.

Voice Communication

There are two ways in which communication may be made with an entity through the voice of the client. The more common one is where the client hears, feels or knows what the spirit wants to say and communicates this to the therapist. The therapist asks questions which are responded to by the entity through the client. The second approach is where the spirit takes over the voice mechanism of the client and speaks directly with the therapist. This can be quite frightening for the client depending on what the discarnate spirit wants to say.

In one case a male spirit used the voice of my client to try to threaten, intimidate and abuse us both. The client had to be reassured that I was aware it was not him that was saying those things to me, but the entity. I told him that he was not to be embarrassed or ashamed by anything that came out of his mouth. Due to the difference in the accent and tone of voice it was quite clear when it was the client and when it was the entity communicating. In this instance we held a three way communication. I spoke with the spirit who communicated directly with me while the client described what he was seeing and feeling.

This angry male spirit had tracked my client from another lifetime many hundreds of years ago and was intent on killing him. The spirit was insistent that he was not going to leave until he had succeeded. He was not concerned that my client had no memory of the previous events that had taken place or that he was now living a completely different life. The entity simply wanted revenge and it seemed impossible to dissuade him of this. After a very long conversation however, the spirit apparently decided that he had had enough and was pretty fed up talking to me and not winning the discussion. He therefore decided he would leave and his wife came to meet him. The client was very amused that I had worn the spirit down just by talking to him until his only way out was to agree to leave!

I was very clear during this session that I was not going to allow the spirit to rattle me in any way. I did not react to his abuse, become angry, fearful or ungrounded. I listened to his arguments and made counter arguments. I presented different view points and asked questions that unsettled him. This is the key to any dialogue with an entity. The therapist must remain calm, focused and in control. You may need to draw upon your own life experiences, those of others, books you have read, techniques you have observed, conversations you have held, teachings you have received. Working with the Beings of Light I am often guided to say things that I might not have thought of or was even unaware that I knew. This also happens when I am teaching, doing psychic readings, carrying out a healing or a spirit release. You too may have had the experience of saying something and then thinking "where did that come from?" Well, it comes in very handy when confronted with a spirit!

Dialogue

In this section I will discuss some of the types of dialogue that can take place in spirit release. When I communicate with an entity I speak as I would to any living person. This means finding suitable words that are understandable while remaining calm, confident and assertive. At times I am required to command or instruct the entity and this needs to be undertaken with an air of authority. Sometimes the dialogue happens telepathically so that the client is not distressed by the content of the communication. At others the conversation happens with or through the client and they will hear everything that takes place. After the release it may be necessary to explain parts of the dialogue which the client may not have understood, but which the spirit did. For example, I have held discussions with spirits about other lifetimes in which possibility the client did not believe. I have also used Universal Laws and esoteric teachings in my conversations with the spirits that may need to be explained afterwards. In this section I will explain the various dialogues that I employ with human and non-human spirits.

Human Spirits

With all human spirits that are attached to living people or places one of the first issues that need to be established is whether they are aware of their situation. I therefore generally ask if they are aware that their physical body has died. Death is so simple and natural that many earthbound spirits have not realized the change that has taken place. If they are aware of their physical death then it is important to establish why they did not subsequently pass into the Light. I have heard various reasons including that they did not see the Light, perhaps because they died while unconscious or during a trauma. Some see the Light, but decide they are not yet ready to die or say that they cannot leave because there is an unresolved issue. I met one lady of ninety two years of age who was haunting a flat. She completely remembered her death and explained she was angry because she was not yet ready to die. She had left the hospital bed, walked down the ward and into the waiting room where she was unable to communicate with her daughter and grandson who were sitting there. She had then decided she would simply go home.

Some spirits tell me that they think they are going to Hell or will be punished in some way for their misdeeds. Others tell me that they are not good enough to go into the Light. In this case it may be necessary to speak with the spirit about what it is they have done. Sometimes it is simply enough to explain that there is no Hell; there is no punishment in the Light. To assure them that no harm will come to them, they have already been forgiven and are merely creating their own Hell where they are. After all an earthbound spirit retains all of their negative emotions, thoughts, distress, pain, disfigurements and disabilities. Once they go into the Light healing takes place and they can find peace. This fact can be used with great effect to persuade a spirit to let go.

Other discarnate humans see people waiting for them who have already passed into Spirit, but do not want to go with them and so turn away from the Light. I was once contacted by someone whose father was dying in hospital. Everyone had expected him to die several days before, but for some reason he kept holding on even though he was in great pain. I was asked if I would do some remote work to find out what was happening. I psychically tuned into the man in his hospital bed and could see a group of spirit people gathered around him. At the front of this group and much closer to him was a rather disheveled woman. It was this lady that he could see waiting for him. I asked if he knew it was his time to pass into spirit and he agreed that it was. I asked why he was unable to let go and glaring towards the woman he retorted "I'm not going with her." I asked why and he explained that she was an ex-wife and he did not want to be with her. I then very gently addressed the woman standing by his bedside, thanked her for coming and explained that he did not want to go with her. I asked her to leave which she did. At this point the rest of the crowd drew forward so that he could see them. I understand from his family that he passed peacefully three hours later.

If the spirit is not aware of their death then I have to explain it to them. This might be done by taking them back to their last memory. They may remember being ill or in an accident. If I can see their death I gently guide them through it as they remember. The trauma of that memory may have to be dealt with. I have spoken with abused children and many others who have been murdered. One young boy of seven told me of a life of beatings by his father who ultimately shot him through the head. The boy was so used to being hurt and in pain that he had assumed this was another time and he would just carry on.

My explanation to the spirits who do not remember their passing is that their physical body has died. Their spirit body however, continues to live on and that is how they are communicating with me. I ask if they have wondered why people have not spoken to them or appeared to see them. With some spirits I have to explain that they are attached to another human being and show them the clothes they are now wearing and the hands they are using. Some spirits find it very confusing to look at the client's hands and realize they are not their own. Male spirits find it particularly disconcerting that they are in a female body and wearing a skirt, for example.

One spirit family I spoke with recently did not believe that there was anything after death. They thought they would just die and be put into the ground. They were continuing in that belief even though clearly existing after physical death. The family had to completely re-evaluate and accept the truth of their situation before they could advance into the Light. It is true that we create our own reality both in life and after death.

In some cases I have found spirits who died in hospital and wandered the wards and corridors. If they find a distressed or very ill child they may attach to that youngster with the intention of looking after them. Unfortunately the spirit can then remain stuck with him/her for many years. In this case the spirit needs to understand the current situation, that the child is now an adult. I always thank them for their care and protection and explain it is now time for them to be looked after in the Light. Some need a bit of encouragement to let go, while others readily accept that they have succeeded in keeping the child safe and their task is done.

In many situations where there are unresolved issues it is a case of working towards resolution and sometimes re-education. My psychotherapeutic training comes in very useful here! In one particularly complicated family situation a client reported that her recently deceased grandfather was keeping her awake at night by making a lot of noise. I connected with him through the client and he explained that he was very unhappy that his daughter-in-law who he did not like now had his wife's wedding ring. The grandfather was very clear who he wanted to have the ring, but as he had died without making a will he had been unable to declare his wishes. We debated for some time and in the end agreed that my client, his grand-daughter, would discuss the matter with her father who could then speak to his brother. I had to facilitate the dead man's arrival at the understanding that this issue may not be resolved in the way that he desired. He had now made his wishes clear and his task was to continue with his journey into the next world. Eventually he agreed to leave his grand-daughter in peace and went into the Light to be with his wife who had passed before him.

Many spirits and clients need to be re-educated with regard to their beliefs, assumptions or understandings. For example, in the case of suicide many believe they are thrown into limbo and wander in the darkness forever or are actually sent to Hell and suffer terrible pain and torment for the rest of time. The person the spirit is attached to may also be consciously holding onto them to prevent this terrible fate. Over years of doing this work I have discovered that reality is actually very different. My understanding is that people who commit suicide go directly into the Light if they so choose. The Light does not discriminate. It is our beliefs, level of distress or unconsciousness that might prevent us progressing as we should. This situation requires a re-education of both the spirit and also the client who is holding on in an attempt to protect that discarnate human. Once this type of spirit passes into the Light they are usually given a lot of healing and I have seen some being escorted to what looks like a hospital room where they can be very well looked after.

I am aware that suicide is an emotive issue for many people. I would like to be clear that it is not for us to judge the actions of another. The therapist needs to remain loving and compassionate despite perhaps their own very different thoughts on suicide. This is the same for many issues that can arise in the area of spirit release including those of abortion, abuse and criminal activity. If you choose not to work with certain issues or situations then this needs to be made clear to potential clients. I have spoken with many spirits and also incarnate people who have committed such deeds and I have to remain non-judgmental and accepting of them. This can be done without condoning the deed itself. We do not know why another person has consciously or unconsciously chosen a certain path. I do know that the majority of spirits regret their actions, feel remorse and want forgiveness.

The release of humans involves directing them to see the Light. I speak to them about the warmth, peace, joy, freedom, forgiveness and healing in the Light. I explain that it is not going to hurt them, even though it is bright it will not blind or burn them. I suggest they feel how beautiful, gentle and loving the Light is. I then encourage the spirit to see a figure in the Light coming towards them. Most spirits see someone they have known in their lifetime and many are overjoyed to be reunited. Others see someone coming who they did not realize was deceased. In this case I explain that the spirit has been wandering for some years and the person who is coming for them is not a trick, but is now in spirit and there to help them on the next part of their journey. Others are not met by anyone they recognize, but there is always a Being of Light who will welcome and look after them. Children are often collected by a parent or grandparent, but in many cases I have given a child into the care of a very beautiful female Light Being who I have grown to know as "the lady who comes for children."

Human spirits may be released together as a group or singly. If there is a family then it is a good idea to keep them together as they go into the Light. Some adult spirits will volunteer to take care of any spirit children also with the client. I have also found groups who have died in the same accident and who can be released at the same time with perhaps a stronger one taking care of the others and communicating with me as to where they are in the process. For example, there might be some who see the Light and others who don't. Those that do see it can be asked to show the others or encourage them to feel it instead. When looking into the Light for someone to come and meet them some spirits will be slower at this than others perhaps caught up in fear that there is no-one for them. The stronger ones in the group or the group leader with whom I am communicating can be called upon to assist. In many cases however, although there is more than one spirit with the client they will not be aware of each other and you will therefore have to work with them separately.

I always ask the spirit if they are happy to go with the person who arrives to meet them. Very occasionally they are not and so we ask for another to come instead. During this process I talk to them about the healing that will take place, how they will lose their pain and become whole again. I speak about the people who love and have come to take care of them. If they are ashamed to face the person who arrives then I explain that this person has already forgiven them. I encourage them to look into the eyes of the person who has come to gauge their feelings. I suggest the spirit reaches out their hand and inform them that their loved one is reaching out to them. Many spirits leave very quickly and easily at this point.

The client may feel or see the release or might simply feel lighter and more peaceful. Some clients experience the grief or fear of the spirit in the early stages. Some cry or feel panic without understanding why. I explain that they are experiencing what the spirit is feeling. After the spirit has departed a few clients have a sense of loss and become tearful. After all they have perhaps lost something that has been with them for a considerable period of time and their energy might feel quite different. This grieving may continue for a few days after the treatment and is quite normal.

Dark & Demonic Spirits

At the beginning of each process once I have established that there is at least one entity on board I ask a set of questions to establish what it is. I usually start with how it identifies itself, for instance is it male or female, is it human, an elemental, a being of the Earth or another dimension, or of the Light. Even if I get the sense of a dark energy I will still ask the previous questions just to make sure. If I have received a negative answer to all of these possibilities I will ask "are you a Being of the Darkness?" If I receive a positive answer at this point I need to establish what type it is. As we have seen before there are a variety of Dark Force Entities commonly known as DFE's. They may range from a limited thought form to the very dark and dangerous. In the earlier section on demons we looked at the varied types of communication that might be held with them. This may range from grunts and growls to threats, claims of "he is mine" and torrents of abuse. So let us look at how the therapist might communicate with these entities.

The low level type of demon can be quite persistent and repetitive in its statements, but is usually quite easy to confuse as it is not generally intelligent. One conversation I frequently hold is to find out what they are supposed to be doing to their victim. I then point out that they have clearly not succeeded in destroying them, killing them or whatever is their intention. I illustrate that here is the client with me, functioning and well (even if they are not) and stress the point that the demon has not succeeded in its endeavors. The demon usually becomes a bit confused at this point and may react with bravado or threats. Anger is the flip side of fear. If an incarnate or discarnate entity reacts with anger then deep down it is afraid. Knowing this helps me to remain compassionate towards an abusive spirit. If there is an angry outburst I will often ask the entity what it is afraid of. This commonly stops it in its tracks although not always! I usually persuade the demon(s) that the client is obviously stronger than they are. The demon is told that it will never succeed and thereby starts to lose its confidence and also its hold on the victim. If I am communicating aloud with the entity then the client hears the conversation. Their growing confidence and awareness of the weakening of the entity assists them in becoming stronger and in their resolve to let it go.

It usually helps to point out that in fact the entity is trapped with the client – it cannot leave unless assisted. Some demons insist that they can leave so you might simply call their bluff and tell them to show you. They of course very quickly realize that what you have pointed out is true. Do not however, try this with an entity that is able to come and go at will unless you know what you are doing. It could leave and you might lose control of the situation while the entity gains in confidence. It may then attach to someone else or re-attach to the client once they have left the session. On the other hand you might succeed in getting the spirit to leave and while a Being of Light deals with it you protect the client to prevent its return. Do not allow an entity to go where it wants to as you are merely passing the problem on to another person to whom it will attach.

Some communication with a DFE is designed to weaken, undermine and confuse while other dialogue is designed to re-educate, encourage and gain its trust. In my view if the therapist tries to bully any entity it will probably become more difficult to deal with. I always work from the premise that if I was a spirit how would I like to be dealt with? I do not respond well to deception, lies, anger or abuse and so neither will a spirit. I was recently told by a woman that she had faced a spirit in her house and had prodded it with a long sharp stick into the "fires of Hell" in an attempt to dispose of it. She had of course not succeeded in releasing the spirit just in making it very angry. I hope one day she is not earthbound and someone treats her in the same way.

I have found that some DFE's will admit to having a master if asked directly. A few however, do not admit it at the beginning, but then you discover at the point of release that they are terrified. In this instance it is useful to establish why they are frightened. It might simply be that they are afraid of being punished or plunged into the legendary "fires of Hell." On the other hand it could be fear that the master will obstruct their release and carry out all of the threats made previously which have held the demon in place. These threats form a very effective way for the master to retain control – through fear. It is unusual to find the master actually in the client's energy field, but it cannot be ruled out as I have discovered some cases in which this was true. I have also found that the master will frequently be aware of the work taking place and may well arrive and try to intervene. You could therefore find yourself communicating directly with the master rather than one of its minions.

Once I have established that there is a master in charge I ask if the master has instructed them to do certain things to the victim which the demon will readily confirm. I ask if the master has promised certain rewards for its efforts which once again is confirmed. I then verify that the demon is doing what the master has instructed. Once we have established this I then ask if the master has provided the rewards promised which of course he hasn't. I explain that the contract between the demon and its master is therefore null and void. It has been broken because one side has not kept to the agreement. The master is in breach of the contract. I also point out that the master has ruled through fear and lies and cannot be trusted. With the demon's confidence in its master undermined it is generally easier to remove.

There are many Dark Masters who are not the Dark One himself. Just as there are many Beings of Light that are not God,

Spirit, the Source or the Divine. Many demons and masters do not profess to having names. There have been sessions however, in which the demon has named its master and will invariably use one of the classic names for the Devil - Satan, Beelzebub, Lucifer and so on. If you are told that the Dark One is the master in this instance you need to be very aware of your protection and the Light that is with you as you work. I usually hold a discourse about the power of the Light over the Dark to reassure the entity, but also the client. It is pretty frightening to hear that the Devil is involved with the spirit you have attached to you.

In this situation I talk about how the Darkness needs the Light and vice versa. The two create balance. The Darkness makes the Light brighter. If you are in a dark place and turn on the light there is no more darkness. If it is dark inside a closed box and you open the lid there is no more darkness. It is dark inside your fridge until the door is opened and the light automatically comes on. In this way then, the Darkness can never overcome the Light. The Light is always stronger, brighter and enduring. We all have Light within us and around us even if it is in differing degrees. We also have darkness within us and around us – our own Shadow.[15]

The Shadow holds our undesirable impulses and inferior personality traits which we have unconsciously hidden away inside of us. The Shadow also holds our potential in that it includes qualities that can become positive through self-awareness. For example, anger can be channeled into energy which can be dynamic, creative and constructive. There is always potential for reconciliation of the unconscious Shadow with the conscious mind - the balance of Darkness and Light.

Many demons will acknowledge at the beginning of the

dialogue that they are beings of the Darkness. Once the demon is confused and in doubt then I start to work on the fact that every being has Light within. This is a technique originated by William Baldwin[16] which I have developed and use very successfully. I persuade the demon to look deep inside and find its own pearl of Light which of course it does. I then work with it to increase that Light and inform the entity that it is indeed a being of Light. I talk to the demon about how we have all come from the Light eons before and therefore need to return to the Light where we belong. I speak of free will, freedom, happiness and peace, being without pain, darkness, coldness, fear or suffering. I demystify the Light as they have frequently been told that it will burn or blind them. I talk of the protection the Light will give them and that they do not need to fear the master as he can no longer touch them. At this point I carry out the release.

If the master however, is a living human who has conjured this entity then I ask for guidance from my team of Light Beings as to the course of action I should take. In this instance I am sometimes advised to return the created or summoned entity to its originator or master. I have found that on asking these entities if they wish to return to their human master they will readily agree. I usually psychically see the person who has carried out this work and they can frequently be identified by the client.

As mentioned in the previous section on demons there are some that are very powerful, intelligent and dangerous. It is this type which will rarely condescend to speak, might physically convulse the client's body and will try to invoke fear and the withdrawal of the therapist. Do not attempt to deal with this if you are not competent to do so. If this type of demon does decide to communicate it is not open to discussion, education or negotiation. As the therapist you can of course choose not to dialogue with any entity. You might decide that it will not achieve anything and therefore focus on performing the clearing.

Contracts

A contract is an agreement made between at least two parties. As we have seen above, it usually involves at least one party agreeing to do something for a reward of some kind. If you know the Faust story by Goethe[17] then you will be aware of the ultimate contract. Faust sold his soul to the Devil in reward for knowledge and power. In Faust's case the Devil provided the knowledge and power for twenty four years before Faust had to relinquish his soul at the point of death. In that event Faust was saved by the Angels and therefore did not lose his soul and the Devil was furious.

In my work I have discovered a number of people who have at some time in their existence made a pact with the Darkness. More commonly, negative agreements are made through the darkness of ourselves or another. For example, contracts are often made in order to gain power over another person, situation or property. They are generally formed through feelings of anger, greed, jealousy, hatred, guilt, shame, fear, insecurity and vulnerability. Contracts do not need to be written and are often verbal. In the past people commonly made a blood pact by cutting a part of the hand or thumb and exchanging blood. This is not a safe practice in the age of HIV, hepatitis and MRSA. Some witchcraft ceremonies involve drinking blood mixed in perhaps a little wine. There are many teen witchcraft books on the market now, some of which encourage this ritual to bind a group of potential young witches together. I personally would not recommend this as a safe activity.

The key to a contract situation is to find out what one party wants from the second party. Has that been provided? What has the second party agreed to do in order to honor this exchange? For example, think of the wedding vows. As part of these vows two people agree to be faithful to one another until their death. This is a positive contract made in love in which both parties are agreeing to be sexually loyal to their partner. The formal document is signed, witnessed and officially recorded. In the event of one of them having an affair then the other can instigate divorce on grounds that their contract has been breached. One of them has not kept the pact. The Court then ends the contract making it null and void which releases both people from the agreement made on their wedding day.

In contract work with clients or with entities it has to be ascertained what was agreed and whether that agreement has been kept. The contract between master and demon that I find most frequently is one where the master has made the demon agree to reside with a human host. While with the human the demon must cause as much damage and chaos as possible. In some cases the contract might include illness, disability and even death. The master agrees that if the demon succeeds he will provide a reward. Invariably this is power or freedom or in one case the demon told me that the Dark Master had promised eternal life! Once I have ascertained this information I ask if the master has ever rewarded the demon which of course he hasn't. I work on the fact that this demon may have been with its human host for some time and yet the master still has not paid. The demon may well have been with other hosts before this one, maybe having succeeded in causing considerable harm. The master still has not paid up and yet the demon continues to do the master's bidding. I point out how unfair this is and that the master obviously has no intention giving what he has promised. At this juncture the demon is usually quite ready to end the contract.

Ending a contract whenever it has been made is quite simply achieved once the client or entity understands the issue. The power of a contract is very strong while at least one party believes in it. The stronger of the two parties will not believe in the contract if they have no intention of providing the promised reward. The stronger one however, will use the weight of the contract to threaten or intimidate. "You must continue to do what I want or I will harm/kill you." The weaker party believes in the threats and must therefore do whatever they have agreed to. Once the weaker party knows that the stronger one will not reward them then they need to understand that they cannot be harmed if they fail to meet their side of the bargain.

One of the important issues for an entity in this position is to trust that the therapist is able to protect them from the master. It must believe that the therapist is able to prevent the master from carrying out his threats. Ultimately the spirit release therapist is offering the entity a way out. I speak to the entity about being free and unafraid instead of being trapped in the dark and cold. In the case of the entity that had been promised eternal life I pointed out that his Dark Master did not have that power. Every being has the gift of eternal life anyway so he had lied. I talk to them about the power of the Light as opposed to the power of the Darkness and assure them that the Light will protect them. These entities are often quite easily persuaded by a therapist who talks to them kindly and honestly. In this way I have never had an entity ultimately refuse to go to the Light through fear that their master will reach them.

A contract ends when one of the two parties decides that it will. It is impossible to maintain a contract alone. When working with clients who have made one during their various lifetimes I facilitate their understanding of the nature of the contract and then the termination. Sometimes we might visualize a paper document and a few people are able during their visualization to read the written words including the date. This contract might be burned in a fire. Sometimes it is enough for the person to say aloud "I terminate any contracts I have made in the past which no longer serve me." On other occasions to add to our completion of contract termination we might use the phrase "I give back all that is yours and take back all that is mine" as utilized in a decording technique.

After the session the client needs to change any behavior, patterns of thought or emotion that were a part of the agreement which has been ended. If for example, their contract bound them to an abusive situation then that needs to be addressed. In one case a woman had formed a contract in a previous life with the person who was now her mother. In the former life their roles had been reversed and my client, as the parent, had experienced the guilt of not being able to protect her child. The child, now the client's mother, had died. The contract formulated meant that the client had agreed to protect her mother in this life from any harm and ultimately death. From very early childhood she had endeavored to keep her mother safe while the latter was often intent on doing everything she could to put herself and her children at risk. This created an impossible situation in which the client was anxiously tied to her mother and now facing the death of her ageing parent. The client was unable to explain the extent of her anxiety and terror around the impending demise. She was bewildered that she did not like her mother yet felt an extraordinary sense of duty to her. Understanding the contract and terminating it released my client from her dread of failure to keep her ailing mother alive forever. It released both of them from historic and unattainable expectations.

CHAPTER 9

WORKING WITH GUIDES, ANGELS AND ASCENDED MASTERS IN SPIRIT RELEASE

Each of us has a personal Guide who is with us from birth until our passing into Spirit. Some people prefer to relate to a Guardian Angel instead. In addition to this Being we also have access to many other energies which can help us in our daily lives. I communicate with a whole range of Guides, Angels and Ascended Masters who assist me in healing, medical intuitive and psychic work, psychotherapy, teaching and writing as well as with the more prosaic issues of finding parking spaces and specific items in the supermarket! You might choose to work for example, with a Guide on a business project, with an Angel for self healing or with an Ascended Master such as Serapis Bey to help you with an addiction to perhaps chocolate or cigarettes.

So what are the differences between these three energies? A Guide is a Being who was once incarnate, meaning that they have lived a physical life here on Earth. Guides therefore understand what it is to be human and are part of the human stream of consciousness. As a Guide they now have an objective overview of the situations in which you might find yourself. A Guide does exactly what is implied – it guides and assists. It does not force you into a course of action or go off in a huff if you decide to take a different route. We all have free choice. If you find yourself working with an energy that aggressively instructs, threatens, bullies and sulks then it is not a Guide and needs to be firmly sent away.

There are many levels of Guides who bring a wide variety of skills, resources and ways of communicating. Numerous Guides appear to us in a personified form, but others appear as color or as a feeling. Some will be very practical, others will be creative and assist with the production of music or art, some will offer teachings and knowledge, others will protect the house or people. They might communicate in words, pictures, colors, feelings, touch, smell, taste or through knowing and sensing. Later in this chapter I will describe how to safely connect with a Guide.

An Angel is a Being that has never been incarnate apart from the two exceptions of Sandalphon and Metatron. All Angels apart from these two have names ending in "el" meaning "of God" in Hebrew. For example, the names of the four well known Archangels - Michael, Raphael, Uriel and Gabriel all end in this way. The Archangels Sandalphon and Metatron are different because they did once live upon the Earth. Sandalphon is said to have been the prophet Elijah who ascended to heaven in a fiery chariot. Metatron is thought to have been Enoch, a prophet and scribe who is now thought by some to be in charge of the Akashic records.[18]

Angels have a higher vibration than Guides and may therefore be experienced in a different way. If we accept the fact that Angels have never been or ever will be incarnate then it follows that neither humans nor Guides will ever become Angels. There are different levels of Angels just as there are Guides. So you may have heard of the Archangels, Seraphim, Cherubim, Thrones, Dominions, Virtues, Powers and Principalities.[19] We can also call upon the Angels that represent qualities such as peace, beauty, justice, and love. In addition there are Angels that take care of and protect a particular place or community.

The Ascended Masters were once great spiritual teachers, prophets or healers in their time and continue now to help us from the Spirit World. They arise from all cultures, religions and civilizations and include New Age masters as well as those from myth and legend such as Merlin. Some of the most famous are Jesus, Mother Mary, Moses, Saint Germain, Buddha, Krishna, Ganesh, Kali, Horus, Kuan Yin and Babaji in addition to various other saints, devas, deities, gods and goddesses. All Ascended Masters may be called upon for guidance and assistance and each has specific issues, goals, aspects or qualities that may be of help in certain situations.[20]

I have described in chapter 8 how I call upon and work with the Beings of Light in a spirit release session. In this chapter I will explain the various Beings with whom I have worked and how they can assist. All of the following might be summoned specifically by name or may attend of their own accord as appropriate. At the beginning of a session I may not know whose help it is that I need so I generally let Spirit decide.

Guides

In a spirit release session I will work with a whole range of Guides with different roles and abilities. My personal Guide is always with me and constantly available. He is multi-tasking and very practical as well as providing guidance and protection. In addition my Committee of Seven are always in attendance when I am working. They provide me with the psychic information I need to do the job. For instance, it is they who show me the person sending a psychic attack and how it has been carried out.

Other Guides come and go as I need them so they will not all attend every session. I have one group of warriors and another of hooded beings who will overcome and surround a difficult entity and escort it away. Both of these groups ensure that the entity is taken through one of the astral doorways, is kept safe and cannot return. At times I work with a group I call the "social workers." Having spent twenty five years in social work myself I felt this was very appropriate! This particular group takes care of a spirit that is fearful and not yet ready to leave. Once I have explained that the spirit cannot stay where it is the social workers take care of them. The spirit is taken to a resting place, given counseling, healing and support until they are ready to move into the Light.

After any entities, curses or cords have been released from a person my healing Guides then arrive. They assist me in healing the aura and chakras and in grounding and protecting the client.

Angels

I am often aware of a large angelic presence while I am working to release spirits. I rarely see personified figures as with Guides, but feel a group energy and sometimes see or sense Light and color. With the Archangels however, I am able to distinguish one from the other by sight and sense. I will go on to describe the Archangels with whom I frequently work during a spirit release session.

Archangel Sandalphon

I first met Sandalphon when working with Archangel Michael to release a difficult entity. He appeared as a very large powerful figure shrouded in black who quickly resolved the situation and removed the spirit into the Light. It all happened so fast that I did not have time to check him out, but was reassured by Archangel Michael that he was a good guy! It is often the case that we fear any spirit that appears to us as dark and does not show any features. I have discovered in the work that I do that I cannot judge a spirit by how it appears just as none of us can judge another human being by their appearance. It is a case of getting to know them and their energy. So when Sandalphon approaches now I recognize and welcome him as a powerful friend to have in this work. If I specifically call him he arrives promptly and will do whatever is needed. His energy at times feels gentle, but at others can feel very strong. Some people report hearing music when Sandalphon is near. He is particularly good at working with extra-terrestrials as well as the negative entities. I sometimes call upon Sandalphon and Melchizedek together as the two most powerful forces to deal with the demonic spirits.

Archangel Michael

It is estimated that around 600,000 people call upon Archangel Michael every minute of every day. He responds to all of those calls. One group exercise that I sometimes carry out with a class is to summon one of the Archangels to stand in the center of the group and then ask the energy to also stand behind each individual.

The students are amazed that an Archangel can be everywhere at once and that each of them can have a very special and individual connection to that Being at the same time. You can be assured that every time you summon Archangel Michael he will be with you.

Sometimes I see Michael with his sword pointed upwards and sometimes it is pointed down to the Earth. Once I saw him on horse back and I regularly see the color blue when he is present. I find he is excellent at working to release human spirits who are resistant to leaving. He uses his sword to sever any attachment or cording and also to protect myself and the client. Many people call upon Michael for protection in various situations.

Archangel Raphael

Raphael is the healer. A healer of the planet Earth, people, animals and plants. I always experience him as a huge energy which at times feels gentle and at others quite strong depending on what is needed. He will often work with Archangel Michael in removing spirits. Raphael can also be asked to assist in the distant healing of another person.

Ascended Masters

I have found that the Ascended Masters tend to arrive during a session with a client whenever they perceive a need. Over the years I have therefore met various Beings of whom I was not previously aware. Once they have indicated to me who they are I have often had to go away and find out a bit about them. Some of these Beings I have only met and worked with on one occasion while others are regular co-workers. In this section I plan to include the Masters with whom I have personally worked as well as others who you may also find helpful in the areas of spirit release and protection.

It is important to say here that in working with the various Ascended Masters or Archangels you should have the confidence to trust your own insight. There are many books describing how a specific Master or Angel appears and it is very easy to lose confidence if the energy you connect with does not match a written description. For example, some experience the color red when they connect with Kuan Yin. Whenever I work with her I always perceive the color yellow. This does not mean that anyone is wrong or connecting with a different Being. It just means that we understand her energy differently. Be confident in your own perceptions and senses.

Melchizedek

I first met Melchizedek when I was struggling to release a Dark Force Entity (DFE). I called upon Spirit to send a powerful enough Being that could assist. Behind me arrived an exceptionally huge, dark entity that for an instant gave me concern that I had allowed something in that wasn't a Being of Light. I instantly asked three times if he was from the Light and received very strong responses that indeed he was. I always like to warn students that if they call upon Melchizedek this is the energy they can expect to meet.

I quickly learned that Melchizedek does not communicate a great deal during a release. The method we have formulated is that as I stand at the head or the feet of the client on the couch, Melchizedek walks through me and their prone body. As he moves forward their physical body, chakras and energy field are cleared and then Melchizedek leaves as suddenly as he arrives taking any entities with him. Sometimes he will tell me to instruct the client to breathe in deeply and then as they breathe out he removes the entity. On other occasions Melchizedek will overshadow me while we carry out the work.

The energy of Melchizedek is now instantly recognizable to me. If he appears as I am doing my general summoning of the most appropriate Beings of Light at the beginning of the session I know that I am about to encounter a strong, dark and sometimes demonic force attached to the client.

Mother Mary

I found for a couple of years in particular that many female clients had the presence of Mother Mary with them. Through these experiences I came to recognize her gentle, compassionate, loving energy along with the color blue. On one occasion I was working to release a very elderly, frail, confused male spirit from a client when I saw Mother Mary approaching. I waited to see what would happen and she very simply put her arms around him, talking quietly to him and led the man away.

Jesus

Let me elucidate the difference between these three energies. Before working I always connect to Source. By this I mean the source of "all that is." The Light from which we have all come and to which we all return. The source of healing, joy, peace, love, compassion and all other positive energies. You might refer to Source as God, Allah, Yahweh or simply as Spirit, the Divine or the Universe depending upon your beliefs.

Jesus was a man who lived upon the Earth and has become known as an Ascended Master. Many Christians are very familiar with his energy and He may be called upon to assist in many ways including healing. The Christ Light is quite different to the energy of Jesus and of Source and I always sense it as white Light. It is a calm, powerful energy that may be called upon in spirit release work just as at any other time.

Horus

Another energy that has arrived during a spirit release session was that of Horus. Horus is of Egyptian origin and is seen with a falcon's head which has one all-seeing eye. The occasion on which he appeared in my therapy room was to resolve a past life issue in Egypt experienced jointly by the client and accompanying spirit. Horus assisted in that resolution and in the peaceful removal of the spirit.

Saint Germain

I have connected with Saint Germain many times, but in only a few occasions of spirit release. The very simple way to recognize his energy is the violet flame or color that you might see or sense when he is present. The violet flame can be used very effectively to cleanse and transmute energy, changing it from negative to positive.

Other Ascended Masters

In addition to those above with whom I have personally worked there are various others that you might connect with to help you in releasing negative energies or with protection. Doreen Virtue's book, *Archangels and Ascended Masters*[21] provides a variety of suggestions. Do remember to make your own connection and form your own perceptions of each.

Some examples that you might like to call upon in spirit release work include **Kuan Ti**, a Chinese warrior god who helps to clear the lower energies; **Sanat Kumara**, a Hindu warrior god devoted to clearing negative entities; **Solomon** who is mentioned in various ancient texts as banishing demons; **Ashtar** who works to protect the Earth from negative extra-terrestrials; or **Anubis** the Egyptian jackal headed god who helps souls in their transition.

For protection you might like to try **Athena**, **El Morya**, **Ishtar** or **Kuan Yin**.

Exercise To Connect With A Guide, Angel Or Ascended Master

The following exercise may be used to connect with any Guide, Ascended Master or Angel, but there may be some differences. This is due to the fact that many people tend to perceive a personified image of a Guide and receive a communication. When we connect to Angels or even Ascended Masters this might not happen in the same way as we are dealing with different energies as previously described. When connecting with an Angel or Master you may therefore see a color or feel an energy rather than perceive a visual image. In addition you may or may not receive a specific message or guidance.

The main emphasis in the process I am about to describe is one of safety. It is absolutely essential to ensure that you are connecting and communicating with a Being of Light and not a lower energy that could cause considerable difficulty. The format includes grounding, opening the chakras, connection to a Being and a check of their origin. I then facilitate a specific

communication with suggested questions followed by disconnection, closure and grounding. I have broken up the process
into different parts which may be used as separate exercises,
perhaps to ground or to attune, for example. It is suggested that you
read the instructions first before trying the exercise. You might
prefer to tape record the words for yourself.

Grounding

First of all ensure that you are sitting in a comfortable, relaxed
position with your eyes closed and your feet flat on the floor. Bring
the focus of your attention to the bottom of your spine. Now imagine that you are sending an anchor from your spine deep into the
Earth on a very long cord, rope or chain. As it drops deeper and
deeper into the Earth you might feel as if your spine is growing
longer or pulling slightly downwards. Now bring your focus to
your feet. Imagine dropping two anchors one from each foot deep
into the Earth on very long cords, ropes or chains. As the anchors
drop deeper and deeper you may feel as if your legs are pulling
downwards. They might feel heavy and your feet may feel as if
they are stuck to the floor. You are now grounded; your body is
heavy and relaxed.

Opening the Chakras

Imagine the energy of the Earth flowing up your legs and into
the red Base chakra at the bottom of the spine. You might feel
this as a pulsing or as waves of energy flowing into the body.
Imagine the Base center opening and expanding. Now bring your
focus up to your orange Sacral center, just below your tummy
button inside the body, allowing this also to open and expand. You

may perceive a feeling of expansion of the lower abdomen and of the lower back. Come up to the yellow Solar Plexus at the diaphragm, feeling this area and the middle of the back relax as the chakra opens. This is the center for sensing or clairsentience. Now bring your attention up to the Heart chakra in the center of the chest, the color of spring green. As the Heart expands feel it open at the front of your chest and also out between the shoulder blades at the back. Many Guides connect with us through the back of the Heart center which is the chakra for our intuition and knowing. Bring your focus now up to the Throat chakra, the color of sky blue. Feel the expansion of the neck and throat. This is the center for communication, smell, taste and hearing or clairaudience. Many Guides will connect here. As you focus on your Brow center allow your forehead to relax and feel the expansion of the indigo chakra at the back of the head as well. This chakra is for telepathic communication and seeing or clairvoyance. Some Guides connect here to communicate through images and color. Come up to the violet Crown center now. This is your connection to the Source, the Divine, the Universe or however you choose to acknowledge that power. Feel the Crown as it opens at the top of your head. You might notice a tingling sensation and a feeling of expansion upwards.

Attuning

Now take your focus up as high as you can. Imagine that you are traveling up through the Universe to a point of white Light; the Source of "all that is." As you connect with that Light allow it to flow down through and around you, welcoming that Light as it fills and surrounds you, bringing a sense of peace, clarity and protection.

Connecting to a Being of Light

Feeling relaxed, grounded and protected it is now time to connect to a Guide, Angel or Ascended Master. If you would like to summon a particular energy such as a known Guide with whom you are already familiar, Archangel Michael or perhaps Babaji, then you may call for that Being specifically by name. You might call upon your personal Guide or one that can help you in a particular way. Otherwise you can ask mentally or out loud for the highest, most appropriate Guide to connect with you.

The Guide, Angel or Ascended Master will approach from behind and you will probably sense a change in your energy or body. These changes can be quite subtle. You might for example, feel coolness or warmth, a tingling or a pressure. You may feel very calm or filled with love or joy. You might want to ask this Being to move around to the side or front of you, to touch your shoulder or hand. If there is a sensation which you don't like such as the feeling of a cobweb on the skin, then ask the Guide, Angel or Ascended Master to change this. If it is too cold for example, then ask for warmth or vice versa. It is important to communicate what you need. As you are trying to establish a connection to this Being then they too are working to make a good connection with you.

Safety Check

Once you have made the initial connection then it is time to check out this Being. This is done very simply by asking the same question three times. The question to ask is "are you of the Light?"

If this Being is not of the Light you will receive a very definite "no" answer by the time you have asked all three questions. This is not a common event and is nothing to be worried about. If however, you do receive a negative answer then quite simply tell the entity very firmly to go and it will do so. Once it has gone you start again by asking for the most appropriate and highest Being of Light to connect with you.

The majority of Beings with whom you connect in this way will be from the Light. The answers you may receive could include a very clear verbal "yes" or "I am of the Light" or "I am Light." You might be shown a flash of Light or receive a feeling of love or warmth. You may simply experience a knowing that this energy is a positive, loving one.

Another way to check out an energy that connects with you is to look into its eyes if they are shown to you. If the eyes stay the same and you sense a loving presence then it is OK. If the eyes change in a negative way then send it away as it is not a Being of Light.

Do not be afraid to send an energy away if you are in doubt. If it is a true Being of Light it will not mind and will understand your hesitancy. It is always better to be safe than sorry.

Getting to Know This Being of Light

Once you are sure that you have connected with a good energy then allow yourself to receive information. Do you sense or see what this Being looks like? Is it male, female or genderless? Does this energy seem old, young or ageless? How would you describe the personality or character of this Being? Do they have a name for you to use? How can this Being of Light assist you in your life?

How will they communicate with you? How will you recognize this energy again? Is there a symbol, color or feeling that you might associate with them? There are many questions which you might ask on this or subsequent occasions.

Disconnection

Once you have finished your communication with the Guide, Angel or Ascended Master then it is time to disconnect. Thank this Being for working with you and ask them to depart. As they leave focus on your own energy, body and grounding. It is at this point that many people feeling the Being of Light depart know that there was an energy with them that perhaps they were not sure about before.

Grounding and Closing Down

Ensure you are firmly grounded by re-checking that your three anchors are deep into the Earth from your spine and feet. Then starting at the Crown chakra imagine gently closing a door across the top of the head. This desensitizes and protects the chakra. Close a door at the Brow center and then at the Throat. Very gently close the door at the Heart remembering that you are just desensitizing and protecting this energy. When you reach the Solar Plexus close this door very firmly, lock it three times with three different keys in three different locks. Then put a shield of golden Light in front of your door to give it added protection. Come down to the Sacral center and close the door. When you reach the Base center keep this red center open and expanded. Fill and surround it with Light for protection and then extend that Light down into the Earth. This means that the Base center is always able to receive energy from the Earth which keeps your body healthy and strong.

Surround yourself in a Bubble of Light which should be about half a meter or eighteen inches from your body all the way round and up above your head. Your Bubble should extend about two meters or six feet below your feet. This is your Bubble of protection and you may keep it filled with Light or imbue it with a color or colors which suit you.

After a connection with a Guide, Angel or Ascended Master you might like to record the event in a journal of some kind to which you can add on successive occasions.

In the next chapter we will explore other techniques for grounding and protection that you might prefer to use instead of those described above.

CHAPTER 10
ENERGY MANAGEMENT

Each of us has to take responsibility for the management of our own energy. Although I have always had natural psychic abilities I did not know anything about grounding, chakras, closing down or protecting myself until I first went to the College of Psychic Studies in London one Sunday afternoon. Some months before my homeopath, who had been successfully treating me for a very long illness, had suggested I go to the College, but I had done nothing about it. I saw advertised in the program a two hour workshop with Ivy Northage, a very famous medium who worked at the College for many years and has since passed into spirit. I felt very drawn to go and witnessed Ivy demonstrating various skills such as aura reading and psychometry amongst others. I sat there with interest, but thinking "I can do that."

It wasn't until the end of the workshop that I really knew why I had been guided to attend. Ivy said that we would all close down before we left. I had no idea what she meant, but participated in a grounding, closing and protection exercise along with the rest of the group. At the end when I opened my eyes I was astounded. The world looked, felt and sounded completely different! I realized that this was how everyone else lived. During a large part of my life I had been completely psychically open, making me far too sensitive. As a result of this and various other reasons I had become very ill and exhausted. In that workshop I learned I had a choice and that I did not have to continue through the rest of my life in the same way. To this day I thank Spirit in the form of Ivy Northage for that very first experience which helped me to regain my health, to focus on my spiritual development and ultimately teach others how to manage their energy too.

If you follow the ideas, concepts and exercises in this chapter on a regular basis you may find that life becomes easier, your body can be healthier and stronger and you will be able to choose when to be "open."

Opening and Closing

The basic concept is that before working psychically, spiritually or in healing we "open up." This means to open the chakras and expand the energy field or aura. Once we have finished working we then "close down." However, these terms can be a little misleading if they are taken literally. A chakra is an energy vortex which is constantly moving and working on many different levels simultaneously. For example, each chakra relates to organs and systems of the body as well as life issues, qualities and emotions. It is impossible therefore to actually close our chakras because they are energy vortices. Energy needs to flow and as healers are aware, if energy becomes blocked or stuck then spiritual, emotional, psychological and physical disease can follow.

Instead of "closing" our chakras it is more appropriate to think about de-sensitizing them. In this way as you come to the end of your meditation or healing during which you will have naturally expanded your energy field and chakras you focus on contracting the energy. Some people do this by ensuring they are aware of their body and the environment around them. Others focus on each chakra and sense them becoming smaller and more contained working from the Crown down to the Base center. Many people use visualization such as imagining flowers closing at the chakra points. In the previous chapter there is an exercise you may use to open up and to close down. In that example I use colors at each of the chakras to open up and doors to close.

I always take extra care when closing the Solar Plexus chakra. This is where we can take on other people's issues – their physical, mental and emotional sensations and so on. Many psychic attacks are directed to this chakra as the Solar Plexus is linked to the digestive system and an attack here can cause severe pain, vomiting, diarrhea, bloating and weight loss. This is also the most commonly corded chakra because it is related to control and power. If closing a door at the Solar Plexus I suggest locking it three times and putting extra protection of a door or gate in front of it. If using a flower or a color to close you might encircle this closed chakra in Light to give it added protection. You may find that one of your other chakras is particularly vulnerable and decide to use added protection there as well. You can be as creative as you like to establish a method with which you feel confident.

Personally I never close the Base center because my reason tells me that this is the chakra which connects us to the Earth and therefore keeps us strong, healthy, energized and grounded. The Base chakra governs the immune system, physical health and the skeletal system. I therefore suggest keeping it open, but surrounding it in Light for protection. Some people however, advocate closing the Base center along with all other chakras. I also advise closing the Crown center whereas others feel happier keeping theirs open. Some sensitives do not work with the chakra system at all and don't believe in opening up or closing down. As in all cases it is important to do what feels right for you. What resonates with you? How does your body feel using one technique as opposed to another? It is a case of finding a method that you like and which works for you. I also advocate having enough confidence to use your chosen system during any class or workshop where the tutor does not close the group down or when a method is used that isn't appropriate for you. Do try other people's techniques as they can add to your understanding and resources. If however, a particular method doesn't suit you then use one that does. As stated at the beginning of this chapter, personal energy management is our own responsibility.

When you want to open up it is actually very simple and people often do it completely naturally and without thought. If you drink a glass of wine you will open up. If you talk or read about spiritual matters you will open up. The key consideration is to be aware of what is happening, where you are and to ensure that you are appropriately protected. You do not want to be sitting in a wine bar enjoying a glass of wine with friends after your psychic development class, talking about spiritual matters and inadvertently take home an energy which is not yours. It is very important that you are aware of when you have become too open in an inappropriate situation and to then close yourself down.

In order to consciously open before undertaking spiritual work many people focus on becoming relaxed, still and centered so that their energy can naturally expand. Some use visualizations such as focusing on the colors of the chakras progressing from the Base center up to the Crown. Others imagine opening flowers or doors or they focus on the feeling of expansion at the chakra points in the body. Once again it is up to you to find a method and pace that suit.

Some people like to take their time to open or to close while it is perfectly possible to complete this in two seconds. To me it is a bit like having an internal switch – I switch it on and off at will. Invariably I am stopped in a corridor between classes for a "quick question" such as "do I have something attached to me?" On such occasions it is quite a simple matter for me to flip the switch on, obtain the answer and turn the switch off again. I do not therefore constantly walk around looking at everyone's auras, chakras or attachments. Apart from maintaining the integrity of my own energy I do not wish to intrude upon anyone else's without their permission.

Grounding

Grounding means to be fully in the body and consciously living in this physical reality. It is absolutely essential to our health and well being. You can tell if someone is not grounded just by looking at them. They often look and feel as if they are not completely present. If you touch them they might not feel very solid and may in fact feel quite frail. In the extreme someone may not just be ungrounded, but actually out of their body. I often see a client's astral body partly separated or in some cases completely detached from the physical body. These people have usually experienced some trauma which has led them unconsciously to disconnect. Living in such an ungrounded or out of the body state means that emotions and physical sensations are numbed and therefore less pain is experienced. It might also mean that the person will be unable to think clearly or make good decisions, they will lose things, forget to eat, have problems with timekeeping, be hyperactive, not listen to what is said to them, receive lots of electric shocks through touching objects or even people, have dizzy spells or blackouts and may also develop bruises while not remembering how it happened. If you recognize the above symptoms in yourself then work on your grounding!

The exercise in the previous chapter contains a section on grounding which may be used on its own. I generally teach people to use anchors from their feet and spine as described. Many people have a problem just grounding from the feet and find that doing so from the bottom of the spine in addition provides a stronger sensation. If however, you have a lower back problem and grounding from here causes you discomfort then just ground from the feet or perhaps from the lower abdomen or Sacral chakra. Another popular and successful method is to imagine roots growing deep down into the Earth from the feet and spine. You might like to imagine that you are a tree reaching those roots down into the Earth to absorb the living water and receive vital nourishment. A more grounded energy may also be achieved through conscious, focused physical exercise. By this I mean exercising while remaining focused on what your body is doing and not on the music from your iPod! You could also benefit from practical activities such as gardening, walking the dog and cleaning the house or car. Grounding can be improved through eating foods such as root vegetables and carbohydrates. Crystals in the darker colors of black, grey, brown and red such as obsidian, black tourmaline, hematite, smoky quartz and ruby may be worn or carried in a pocket to help. Other solutions to assist in your grounding include vitamin C, plenty of water, the homeopathic remedies of arnica and oak, Petaltone's Spirit Ground, the Bush Flower essences of Red Lily or Flannel Flower, and the Bach

Clematis essence. In the Aura Soma range of products the Serapis Bey Quintessence will close, ground and protect while the Pomanders of Deep Red, Red and Emerald Green are good for grounding.

When you are well grounded your body will feel more solid and secure. You will generally be more aware of your physicality and your environment. Many people find that they are less likely to absorb other people's energy and therefore do not feel as tired. Good grounding also means that your aura and chakras can become stronger and more balanced. It is something to keep working on. On some days grounding is easier than others. Periodically one method works better than another. People who have been very ungrounded or out of their body for most of their life are not going to initially feel comfortable when grounded. I have worked with clients who after grounding have thought that they would never be able to move their feet again. These individuals need to be reassured that their body is supposed to feel heavy. Grounding needs to be practiced until they feel more comfortable.

Grounding can be carried out anywhere. I have taught air stewards to ground themselves while flying which they find helps with both their energy and jet lag. You can carry out a grounding exercise whether you are lying, sitting or standing. You might choose to do this while standing on grass, but it can also be achieved just as effectively from the 86th floor of the Empire State building. Do not be concerned as one of my students was, that by sending your anchors or roots down into the Earth from the second floor they will hit the people below! Your visualized roots and anchors are purely focused energy and will not harm or affect others. If you feel that the energy in the flat below you is not very positive then I have known people to effectively ground by sending their roots out of the window and down the outside of the building into the Earth. As with any visualization you can be as creative as you wish! It is essential to ground before opening, meditating, giving a healing or a psychic reading. It is also very important to ensure you are well grounded afterwards. I usually suggest that a routine of grounding, closing and protection is carried out at least twice a day - once in the morning before leaving the house and again at night before sleep. You can quickly check and make any necessary changes as you go through your day.

Cleansing

It is essential that we work to keep our energy clear just as it is important to keep our bodies and environments physically clean. This means letting go of any negative emotions and thoughts which produce toxins within the body and affect your auric field and chakra system. It also requires cleansing each of the chakras and the aura on a regular basis. Some people carry this out daily, others practice it weekly or less often. During a meditation or period of relaxation you need only to focus on each chakra in turn. You might visualize or sense the color and shape of each. If the chakra feels or appears to be a good vibrant color without dark patches or irregularities then it is fine. If however, you sense that some cleansing or repair is required then focus on improving the color and shape or use Light to clear each one. While working on the chakras in this way you may find that issues, emotions or thoughts arise. These indicate work needing to be carried out in order to balance the chakras.

The aura may be worked on in a similar way. Acquire a sense of where your aura is around you. How strong or fragile does it feel? Is it a regular shape and an equal distance from the body all the way around? Do you sense any holes or tears in your aura? Is there a dark patch or shape in your energy? Black or grey spots and patches can indicate a trauma or accident in this or other lives as well as emotional hurt, thought forms and spirits. Again you might decide to clear with Light. After grounding you could call upon the Light or your Guides or Angels to heal, cleanse, repair and strengthen your energy field. You might also like to sense how your aura reacts when you feel anger, fear, guilt, depression, joy or love. How do you feel when your aura is close to the body or expanded? In which states does it feel stronger, balanced and protective? If you are holding a lot of anger for example, this affects your energy field and also how other people react towards you. Nicotine, caffeine, alcohol, recreational and medicinal drugs all affect the aura in some way. I am not advocating a perfect and pure way of life unless that is your choice, just an awareness that everything around and within us has the potential to affect our wellbeing. Regular cleansing of the energy field and releasing emotions and thoughts that are harmful to you and others is essential to your health and safety.

I used to experience very severe jet lag symptoms with vomiting, diarrhea, energy loss and disorientation to name but a few. I discovered that in addition to working on my grounding while flying that I needed to work on my aura as well. The aura when traveling at speed stretches out behind us and so becomes thinner and unbalanced. This can cause some of the symptoms of jet lag. While you are getting off your plane in Italy your aura is still traveling across Europe! This can also happen if you travel at speed in a car, train or any other form of transport. I find that if I focus on my aura every twenty minutes or so during a flight I am able to bring it back to me. It feels a bit like snapping an elastic band behind me each time I pull it back. The first time I traveled to Australia from London I warned my friends that I would be in a poor state when they met me at the airport and I should be put to bed and left there for a few days. On the flight I worked every twenty minutes on my aura and grounding. I do not sleep on planes so this was not a problem. On arrival in Sydney my friends were amazed that I had lots of energy, was feeling fantastic and had minimal jet lag! I have continued this practice whenever traveling and have never been as unwell since.

One clearing method I teach students is to use a vortex of white Light either around them to clear the aura, through each of the chakras or within a room to cleanse it. You simply imagine a spinning vortex or tornado of white Light. It does not matter in which direction or with what speed it is spinning. The key to the vortex is the centrifugal force which means that as it spins it collects anything which is no longer needed. Once it has collected everything the vortex is sent off into the Universe or the Earth where the energy is transmuted. If using the tornado to clear each chakra in turn it needs to be quite small and may be used to enter the chakra from the front or back. If using the vortex to cleanse your aura then I usually suggest you start at the front; it reaches from above your head to below your feet and it spins around you before release. To clear your energy channel start the vortex above your head, spin it down through the body and release into the Earth. To clear a room the vortex should be floor to ceiling.

Sometimes once is enough. Sometimes it is necessary to use the vortex three times or more to clear whatever is being worked on. It should be mentioned here that very occasionally a spinning vortex used to clear a room can make an occupying spirit quite agitated or angry. If this happens a more gentle approach needs to be employed.

Some people do not like the spinning sensation of the vortex and prefer instead to use a disk of white Light. For this you imagine a disk of Light above you large enough to cleanse your aura at the same time as your physical body. The idea of the disk is that as it moves downwards it collects anything you no longer need on the underside and fills you with Light at the same time. As with any task your intention is important. With this exercise I suggest that you bring the disk down first to cleanse the body and then release it into the Earth. Imagine a new disk up above your head and allow it to cleanse the chakras as it comes down. Do the same to clear the aura. As with the vortex the disk can be used once or many times to cleanse each area. The disk and vortex are both quick and effective methods which may also be used to clear a room or healing couch between clients.

In chapter 2, I discussed sitting in someone else's energy on a seat or chair. It is possible in this simple act to pick up the previous occupant's emotions, thoughts or pain. Instead of being uncomfortable in that energy you might choose to use the white Light vortex or disk in order to clear the seat. You could also simply impose your own energy on the chair. This means having an awareness of your energy in order to do so. If you are always aware of how your body feels, what is happening for you on an emotional, mental and auric level then you will sense any foreign energy very quickly and be able to deal with it. Knowing and focusing on your own energy will immediately impose your energy onto the chair in which you sit.

Other methods of cleansing include those previously mentioned such as salt baths. In the seventeenth century salt represented the soul and was placed on the pelvis of a deceased person in their coffin to ward off the Devil. You might alternatively visualize standing under a waterfall or white Light, use a spray such as Crystal Clear, Astral Clear, the Alaskan Purification spray or the Bush Flower Space Clearing essence. The Petaltone essences Spring Dawn, Clear Light and the Aura Cleansing Set are all designed to cleanse your energy field. It is possible to program your shower at home so that every time you physically wash you are cleansed energetically. This is simply carried out through verbalizing your intention once a month while in the shower. The Aboriginal and Native American people use smoke to cleanse and protect. Oils or incense such as juniper berry, tea tree, pine or eucalyptus are also useful. You might call upon Guides, Angels or Ascended Masters to help you in cleansing. Various contaminated objects, jewelry, clothing and photographs may also be cleared using an appropriate method.

Protection

A great deal of emphasis is placed upon the idea of protection. Many people including myself teach what I call the "barrier methods." In other words the techniques of imagining bubbles, shields, mirrors, cloaks, pyramids, rings of fire or salt and so on – all of which intend some form of barrier between us and whatever it is we wish to protect ourselves from. These methods are very practical as they give something tangible to work with and develop confidence in. Whatever method you choose requires the intention and strong sense of knowing that you are protected otherwise it may not be completely effective.

Ultimately however, protection is simply a heightened awareness and deeper connection. So let's look at this concept – what does it mean? In my mind if someone is very aware of their energy, their physical, emotional, mental and spiritual bodies as well as their environment plus they have a deep understanding and connection to the Earth and the Source then they are protected. All that is needed in addition to this is to *know* that you are protected. To me knowing is more than believing. A belief can imply some doubt – "I believe this idea until it is proved otherwise." Whereas knowing is to have an absolute faith and to know in every fiber of your being that something is true. Carl Jung was asked in a BBC interview with John Freeman in 1959 if he believed in God. His answer was "I don't believe. I know." In the same way I know I am protected without question. I rarely use a barrier protection technique even while carrying out a spirit release. My intention and knowing is sufficient. Having said that it has taken me some time to get to this point and I previously used the various barrier methods I teach. So please don't stop using the practices that work for you, but do work towards having an absolute knowing in your safety and wellbeing.

Fear is the enemy of any protection technique as it creates weakness, vulnerability and doubt. In one spirit release class a student related how an earthbound spirit tried to attach to her late one night while she was walking home. She was a good student who was aware of her energy and therefore knew the moment the spirit tried to attach. She immediately dealt with it by keeping the spirit out of her aura. As she walked up the road she knew it was not with her, but as she arrived at her front door a doubt crept in – "has it really gone?" Immediately the spirit jumped on board and she spent the next hour or so releasing it from her flat. Protection should not be based in paranoia or fear; it is about empowering and maintaining a clear, strong energy.

There are various other techniques that can be used to assist you in protecting yourself and becoming confident in doing so. In addition to the various barriers many use symbols such as the crucifix or equal sided cross, the ankh, eye of Horus, hand of Fatima, a flaming torch, a pentagram or pentacle, the star of David, tree of life or any other symbol that has meaning for you. You may be aware for example, of the Maori symbol Manaia which protects from negativity and accidents. Manaia has a bird head, man's body and a fish tail which together represent the balance between sky, earth and sea. Any symbol may be worn or placed in front, behind, above and/or below a person, chakra or object. Some people carry a talisman, a holy book, a phial of holy water or the Kabbalah *Book of Healing and Protection.*

You may find that some colors feel more protective for you than others. Both electric blue and violet can ward off negativity and in some cases earthbound spirits. White Light, silver and gold are frequently used as they are reflective and therefore any unwanted energy is deflected. Archangel Michael is regularly called upon for protection with his sword. You might also choose to call upon a personal protector Guide to be with you.

A very effective technique that I teach to people who are having great difficulty closing down or are under extreme and continuous psychic attack is that of the diver's helmet. If you imagine putting on a diver's, or alternatively an astronaut's, helmet it will cover your Crown, Brow and Throat chakras. You might also choose to take this further and imagine clothing yourself in the diver or astronaut suit, gloves and heavy boots. Not only will the complete suit and helmet protect all of your chakras and energy bodies, but it will keep you grounded. Try it for yourself and see how it feels.

Protective crystals include black tourmaline which creates a psychic shield around you if worn or kept in a pocket. Obsidian, amber, amethyst, jade, jet, carnelian and sodalite will all absorb and help clear negative energy. Rose quartz has a very gentle healing energy while labradorite works to ground, heal and strengthen the aura. Australian Bush Flower essences such as Fringed Violet may be used to strengthen and protect the aura while Angelsword can be used to clear psychic attack and protect. The essential oil of yarrow is very pungent and protective and is similar in smell and usage to the Ghanaian oil Sasorabia. In the Alaskan essences the Guardian spray protects. The Petaltone essences of Release and Aura Flame both clear and protect.

You will also find that simply expanding your energy can enhance your protection when on crowded public transport, for example. Another very useful tip is to focus into your Heart energy and allow that to expand. Not only does it give you a sense of peace, love and compassion, but it can spread to others around you.

Ultimately if you feel out of your depth in managing your energy then do not be afraid to call for assistance – either from the Beings of Light or from a healer or tutor.

Exercise To Raise Your Vibration

To end this chapter on energy management I offer an exercise aimed at heightening the vibration and frequency of your energy field. Negative energy vibrates at a slower, lower rate and is quite dense. The more you raise and speed up your own vibration the lighter and finer your energy becomes and the less likely you are to be affected by the heavier, slower energies. In addition to working on yourself to cleanse your chakras and aura and let go of any negative emotions and thoughts you might like to practice this simple exercise on a regular basis. You can set aside five minutes or half an hour to do this depending on the time available.

Ensure you are sitting comfortably and are suitably relaxed. Imagine your feet are gradually sinking down into the Earth. They feel warm and safe. Allow your legs to sink down until they are in the Earth as far as feels comfortable to you. This might be up to your ankles, your knees or up to your thighs. Allow the Earth to take your weight. Feel the Earth supporting you and accept the energy of the Earth flowing up into your feet and legs and on up into the body. Notice how this Earth energy feels and the effect it has upon you.

Once you are properly grounded take the focus of your attention as high up into the Universe as you can. Imagine traveling higher and higher until you see or sense a distant point of Light. The Light of the Divine, the Light of the Source of all healing, love, joy, compassion and peace. Hold the intention of connecting with that Light and acknowledge it as it flows down towards you. Accept it flowing into your body through the Crown center, filling your body with Light. Notice how this Light feels and the impact it has upon you.

Focus on the energy from the Earth and the energy of the Source as they flow into your Heart chakra in the center of your chest. Feel your Heart chakra expand very easily and naturally as it fills with Light. Connect with that Light deep within you sensing it grow more and more. Allow your Heart chakra to expand and fill with love, peace and joy. Now continue to increase that Heart energy through the body filling the body with those wonderful feelings. Feel the Light flow down into your fingertips and your toes. Sense it flowing through every part of your body.

Now expand that energy from your Heart center through the boundary of the physical body and out into the aura. Make sure that the Light is now filling and surrounding you. It is above your head and below your feet. It is out behind you as well as in front of you and out to both sides.

As you sit now surrounded and filled with the Light notice that your energy field feels lighter and finer. Observe that it is vibrating at a slightly faster speed and higher frequency. The more Light you bring into your energy field the more you are able to enlarge your Heart energy and aura. While maintaining your strong grounding your energy body is also expanded with the sense of a deep connection to "all that is."

Once you are ready to end the meditation, allowing the Light to remain surrounding you, gently contract your Heart energy back into the body and then into the Heart center. Check that your aura is contracted to about half a meter or eighteen inches all around you. It should be the same distance above your head and extended about two meters or six feet under you. Ensure you are properly in the body – that you can feel all parts of your physical body, you can hear the sounds around you and are fully aware of the seat on which you are sitting and the floor beneath your feet. Imagine your legs and spine rooted down into the Earth. When ready open your eyes and notice whether your surroundings look any different. You may find the colors are more vibrant and objects seem in sharper focus. Notice how you feel on a physical, emotional, mental and spiritual level after the exercise.

Managing your own energy is enjoyable as well as beneficial for your health and well-being. In working on your aura, chakras, grounding and protection you can learn a great deal about yourself and your environment. Enjoy and be safe.

USEFUL CONTACTS

College of Psychic Studies
16 Queensberry Place
London
SW7 2EB
England
Tel: 0044 20 7589 3292
Website: www.collegeofpsychicstudies.co.uk

Spirit Release Foundation
C/o Myrtles
Como Road
Malvern
Worcestershire
WR14 2TH
England
Tel: 0044 1684 560725
Website: www.spiritrelease.com

Petaltone Essences
P.O. Box 354
Weston-Super-Mare
BS23 2ZX
England
Tel: 0800 8495036
Website: www.petaltone.co.uk

FURTHER READING

Ashworth, David, *Dancing with the Devil*, (2001), Crucible Publishers, UK.

Baldwin, William J., Ph.D., *Spirit Releasement Therapy: A Technique Manual*, (1991), (1992 second edition), (1995), Headline Books Inc., USA.

Brennan, Barbara Ann, *Hands of Light: A Guide to Healing Through the Human Energy Field*, (1987), (1988), Bantam Books, USA.

Brennan, Barbara Ann, *Light Emerging: The Journey of Personal Healing*, (1993), Bantam Books, USA.

Crowley, Vivianne, *Jung: A Journey of Transformation*, (1999), Godsfield Press, UK.

Fiore, Edith, Dr., *The Unquiet Dead: A Psychologist Treats Spirit Possession*, (1987), Ballantine Books, USA.

Freedom Long, Max, *The Secret Science Behind Miracles*, (1948), (2002), De Vorss Publications, USA.

Furlong, David, *Working With Earth Energies,* (2003), Judy Piatkus (Publishers) Ltd., UK.

Hall, Judy, *The Art of Psychic Protection*, (1996), (1997), Findhorn Press, UK.

Hall, Judy, *The Crystal Bible: A Definitive Guide to Crystals*, (2003), Godsfield Press Ltd., UK.

Hall, Judy, *Way of Psychic Protection*, (1991), (2001), Thorsons, UK.

Heaven, Ross, *Vodou Shaman: The Haitian Way of Healing and Power*, (2003), Destiny Books, USA.

Ingerman, Sandra, *Soul Retrieval: Mending the Fragmented Self,*

(1991), Harper San Francisco, USA.

Ireland-Frey, Louise, M.D., *Freeing the Captives: The Emerging Therapy of Treating Spirit Attachment*, (1999), Hampton Roads, USA.

Judith, Anodea, *Eastern Body, Western Mind: Psychology and the Chakra System as a Path to the Self*, (1952), (1996), Celestial Arts, USA.

Judith, Anodea, Ph.D., *Wheels of Life: A User's Guide to the Chakra System*, (1987), (2000 second edition), Llewellyn Publications, USA.

Konstantinos, *Vampires: The Occult Truth*, (1996), (2002 edition), Llewellyn Publications, USA.

Marshall, Brenda, (Ed.), *While I Remember: The Life Story of Ivy Northage*, (1999), Light Publishing, UK.

Maurey, Eugene, *Exorcism: How to Clear at a Distance a Spirit Possessed Person*, (1988), Whitford Press, USA.

Nelson, John E., M.D., *Healing the Split: Integrating Spirit into our Understanding of the Mentally Ill*, (1937), (1994), State University of New York Press, USA.

Peck, M. Scott, M.D., *Glimpses of the Devil: A Psychiatrist's Personal Accounts of Possession, Exorcism and Redemption,*(2005), Free Press, USA.

Sagan, Samuel, M.D., *Entity Possession: Freeing the Energy Body of Negative Influences,* (1994), (1997), Destiny Books, USA.

Virtue, Doreen, Ph.D., *Archangels and Ascended Masters: A Guide to Working and Healing with Divinities and Deities*, (2003), Hay House Inc., USA.

White, Ruth, *Working With Guides and Angels*, (1996), (2001),

Judy Piatkus (Publishers) Ltd., UK.

Wickland, Carl, M.D., *Thirty Years Among the Dead*, (1924), (1963 edition), National Psychology Institute, USA.

NOTES

[1] Wikipedia Encyclopaedia, (2006), www.wikipedia.org.

[2] Peck, M. Scott, M.D., *Glimpses of the Devil: A Psychiatrist's Personal Accounts of Possession, Exorcism and Redemption*, (2005), Free Press, USA.

[3] British Broadcasting Company, *Witch Child*, BBC 2, April 2006.

[4] Thompson, Della (Ed.), *The Oxford Compact English Dictionary*, (1996), Oxford University Press, UK.

[5] MIND, UK, (2006), www.mind.org.uk.

[6] National Institute of Mental Health, USA, (2006), www.nimh.nih.gov.

[7] Konstantinos, *Vampires: The Occult Truth*, (1996) (2002 edition), Llewellyn Publications, USA.

[8] Crystal Clear was developed as a space and aura clearing essence in 1993, subsequently followed by Astral Clear which is extra strong. Neither has a scent and is therefore suitable for people who react to smells. See Useful Contacts for details of Petaltone.

[9] Thompson, Della (Ed.), *The Oxford Compact English Dictionary*, (1996), Oxford University Press, UK.

[10] Crystal Clear – see Useful Contacts for details of Petaltone.

[11] Australian Bush and Alaskan Essences – available from shops and the internet.

[12] Hall, Judy, *The Crystal Bible: A Definitive Guide to Crystals*, (2003), Godsfield Press, UK.

[13] Wickland, Dr. Carl, M.D., *Thirty Years Among the Dead*, (1924) (1963 edition), National Psychological Institute, USA.

14 Maurey, Eugene, *Exorcism: How to Clear at a Distance a Spirit Possessed Person*, (1988), Whitford Press, USA.

15 Crowley, Vivianne, *Jung: A Journey of Transformation*, (1999), Godsfield Press, UK.

16 Baldwin, William J., D.D.S., Ph.D., *Spirit Releasement Therapy: A Technique Manual*, (1991), (1992 second edition), (1995), Headline Books, Inc., USA, pp.331-334.

17 Goethe, Johann Wolfgang von, *Faust*, (1954) (1971), Sir Theodore Martin (Trans.), J.M. Dent and Sons Ltd., London.

18 Virtue, Doreen, Ph.D., *Archangels and Ascended Masters: A Guide to Working and Healing with Divinities and Deities*, (2003), Hay House, Inc., USA, p.43.

19 White, Ruth, *Working with Guides and Angels*, (1996), (2001), Judy Piatkus (Publishers) Ltd., London, pp.20-22.

20 Virtue, Doreen, Ph.D., *Archangels and Ascended Masters: A Guide to Working and Healing with Divinities and Deities*, (2003), Hay House, Inc., USA.

21 Virtue, Doreen, Ph.D., *Archangels and Ascended Masters: A Guide to Working and Healing with Divinities and Deities*, (2003), Hay House, Inc., USA.

O

is a symbol of the world,
of oneness and unity. O Books
explores the many paths of wholeness
and spiritual understanding which
different traditions have developed down
the ages. It aims to bring this knowledge
in accessible form, to a general readership,
providing practical spirituality to today's seekers.

For the full list of over 200 titles covering:

- CHILDREN'S PRAYER, NOVELTY AND GIFT BOOKS
- CHILDREN'S CHRISTIAN AND SPIRITUALITY
- CHRISTMAS AND EASTER
- RELIGION/PHILOSOPHY
- SCHOOL TITLES
- ANGELS/CHANNELLING
- HEALING/MEDITATION
- SELF-HELP/RELATIONSHIPS
- ASTROLOGY/NUMEROLOGY
- SPIRITUAL ENQUIRY
- CHRISTIANITY, EVANGELICAL
  AND LIBERAL/RADICAL
- CURRENT AFFAIRS
- HISTORY/BIOGRAPHY
- INSPIRATIONAL/DEVOTIONAL
- WORLD RELIGIONS/INTERFAITH
- BIOGRAPHY AND FICTION
- BIBLE AND REFERENCE
- SCIENCE/PSYCHOLOGY

Please visit our website,
www.O-books.net

SOME RECENT O BOOKS

The Art of Being Psychic
The power to free the artist within
June Elleni-Laine

A brilliant book for anyone wishing to develop their intuition, creativity and psychic ability. It is truly wonderful, one of the best books on psychic development that I have read. I have no hesitation in recommending this book, a must for every bookshelf.
Suzanna McInerney, former President, College of Psychic Studies
1905047541 160pp **£12.99 $24.95**

Journey Home
A true story of time and inter-dimensional travel
Tonika Rinar
2nd printing

A lifeline that has been tossed out from the universe to help tether those lost in the wake of recent world events. If you are willing to open your mind, Tonika will take you on a journey home, to a place that shines bright within each of us...... all you have to do is reach for it. **Amazon**
1905047002 272pp **£11.99 $16.95**

Spirit Release
A practical handbook
Sue Allen

A comprehensive and definitive guide to psychic attack, curses, witchcraft, spirit attachment, possession, soul retrieval, haunting,

soul rescue, deliverance and exorcism, and more. This book is the most comprehensive I have seen on the subject of spirit release. This book is a must for anyone working and dealing with people.
Becky Walsh, presenter of The Psychic Show on LBC
1846940338 260pp **£11.99 $24.95**

Spiritwalking
Poppy Palin
Drawing together the wild craft of the shamanic practitioner and the wise counsel of the medium or psychic, Spiritwalking takes the reader through a practical course in becoming an effective, empathic spiritwalker. In an era blighted by professional mystics, Poppy Palin is the real thing. You can trust her - and what she writes - completely.
Alan Richardson, author of The Inner Guide to Egypt and others
1846940311 320pp **£11.99 $24.95**

The 7 Ahas! of Highly Enlightened Souls
How to free yourself from ALL forms of stress
Mike George
7th printing
A very profound, self empowering book. Each page bursting with wisdom and insight. One you will need to read and reread over and over again!
Paradigm Shift
1903816319 128pp 190/135mm **£5.99 $11.95**

God Calling
A Devotional Diary
A. J. Russell
46th printing
Perhaps the best-selling devotional book of all time, over 6 million copies sold.
1905047428 280pp 135/95mm **£7.99** cl.
US rights sold

The Goddess, the Grail and the Lodge
The Da Vinci code and the real origins of religion
Alan Butler
5th printing
This book rings through with the integrity of sharing time-honoured revelations. As a historical detective, following a golden thread from the great Megalithic cultures, Alan Butler vividly presents a compelling picture of the fight for life of a great secret and one that we simply can't afford to ignore.
From the foreword by **Lynn Picknett & Clive Prince**
1903816696 360pp 230/152mm **£12.99 $19.95**

The Heart of Tantric Sex
A sourcebook on the practice of Tantric sex
Diana Richardson
3rd printing
One of the most revolutionary books on sexuality ever written.
Ruth Ostrow, News Ltd.
1903816378 256pp **£9.99 $14.95**

I Am With You
The best-selling modern inspirational classic
John Woolley
14th printing hardback
Probably the consistently best-selling devotional in the UK today.
0853053413 280pp 150x100mm £9.99 cl
4th printing paperback
1903816998 280pp 150/100mm **£6.99 $12.95**

In the Light of Meditation
The art and practice of meditation in 10 lessons
Mike George
2nd printing
A classy book. A gentle yet satisfying pace and is beautifully illustrated. Complete with a CD or guided meditation commentaries, this is a true gem among meditation guides. **Brainwave**
1903816610 224pp 235/165mm full colour throughout +CD **£11.99 $19.95**

The Instant Astrologer
A revolutionary new book and software package for the astrological seeker
Lyn Birkbeck
2nd printing
The brilliant Lyn Birkbeck's new book and CD package, The Instant Astrologer, combines modern technology and the wisdom of the ancients, creating an invitation to enlightenment for the masses, just

when we need it most!
Astrologer **Jenny Lynch**, Host of NYC's StarPower Astrology
Television Show
1903816491 628pp full colour throughout with CD ROM 240/180
£39 $69 cl

Is There An Afterlife?

A comprehensive overview of the evidence, from east and west
David Fontana
2nd printing
*An extensive, authoritative and detailed survey of the best of the
evidence supporting survival after death. It will surely become a
classic not only of parapsychology literature in general but also
of survival literature in particular. Professor Fontana is to be
congratulated on this landmark study and I thoroughly recommend
it to all who are really interested in a serious exploration of the
subject.* **Universalist**
1903816904 496pp 230/153mm **£14.99 $24.95**

The Reiki Sourcebook

Bronwen and Frans Stiene
5th printing
*It captures everything a Reiki practitioner will ever need to know
about the ancient art. This book is hailed by most Reiki
professionals as the best guide to Reiki. For an average reader, it's
also highly enjoyable and a good way to learn to understand
Buddhism, therapy and healing.* **Michelle Bakar**, Beauty magazine
1903816556 384pp **£12.99 $19.95**

Soul Power
The transformation that happens when you know
Nikki de Carteret
4th printing

This may be one of the finest books in its genre today. Using scenes from her own life and growth, Nikki de Carteret weaves wisdom about soul growth and the power of love and transcendent wisdom gleaned from the writings of the mystics. This is a book that I will read gain and again as a reference for my own soul growth. She is a scholar who is totally accessible and grounded in the human experience.
Barnes and Noble review
190381636X 240pp **£9.99 $15.95**

The Creative Christian
God and us; Partners in Creation
Adrian B. Smith

Enlivening and stimulating, the author presents a new approach to Jesus and the Kingdom he spoke of, in the context of the evolution of our Universe. He reveals its meaning for us of the 21st century.
Hans Schrenk, Lecturer in Holy Scripture and Biblical Languages, Middlesex University.
1905047754 160pp **£11.99 $24.95**

The Gospel of Falling Down
Mark Townsend

This little book is tackling one of the biggest and deepest questions which, unexpectedly, brings us to the foundation of the Christian faith. Mark has discovered this through his own experience of falling

down, or failure. **Bishop Stephen Verney**
1846940095 144pp **£9.99 $16.95**

I Still Haven't Found What I'm Looking For
Paul Walker

Traditional understandings of Christianity may not be credible perhaps they can still speak to us in a different way. Perhaps they point to something which we can still sense. Something we need in our lives. Something not just to make us decent, or responsible, but happy and fulfilled. Paul Walker, former Times preacher of the year, does not give answers, but rejoices in the search.
1905047762 144pp **£9.99 $16.95**

An Introduction to Radical Theology
The death and resurrection of God
Trevor Greenfield

This is a clearly written and scholarly introduction to radical theology that, at the same time, provides a contextualised and much needed survey of the movement. At times and in turns Greenfield is passionate, ironical, polemical and acerbic. An underlying wit surfaces in images that punctuate the text. This work is a significant and valuable addition to the literature available not only on theological writing but also cultural change. **Journal of Beliefs and Values**
1905047606 208pp **£12.99 $29.95**

Tomorrow's Christian
A new framework for Christian living
Adrian B. Smith

This is a vision of a radically new kind of Christianity. While many

of the ideas here have been accepted by radical Christians and lib-
eral theologians for some time, this presents them as an accessible,
coherent package: a faith you can imagine living out with integrity
in the real world. And even if you already see yourself as a "progres-
sive Christian" or whatever label you choose to adopt, you'll find
ideas in both books that challenge and surprise you. Highly recom-
mended. **Movement**
1903816971 176pp **£9.99 $15.95**

Tomorrow's Faith
A new framework of Christian belief
Adrian B. Smith
2nd printing
This is the most significant book for Christian thinking so far this
millennium. If this does not become a standard textbook for theolog-
ical and ministerial education, then shame on the institutions! **Revd**
Dr Meic Phillips, Presbyterian
1905047177 128pp **£9.99 $19.95**

The Trouble With God
Building the republic of heaven
David Boulton
Revised edition
A wonderful repository of religious understanding and a liberal the-
ologian's delight. **Modern Believing**
1905047061 272pp **£11.99 $24.95**

Colours of the Soul
Transform your life through colour therapy
June McLeod
A great book, the best I've read on the subject and so inspirational.
Laura, Helios Centre
1905047258 176pp + 4pp colour insert **£11.99 $21.95**

Crystal Prescriptions
The A-Z guide to over 1,200 symptoms and their healing crystals
Judy Hall
2nd printing
Another potential best-seller from Judy Hall. This handy little book is packed as tight as a pill-bottle with crystal remedies for ailments. It is written in an easy-to-understand style, so if you are not a virtuoso with your Vanadinite, it will guide you. If you love crystals and want to make the best use of them, it is worth investing in this book as a complete reference to their healing qualities. **Vision**
1905047401 176pp 2 colour **£7.99 $15.95**

Grow Youthful
David Niven Miller
A practical, extensive guide covering everything you can do to avoid ageing.
1846940044 224pp **£10.00 $19.95**

The Healing Power of Celtic Plants
Healing herbs of the ancient Celts and their Druid medicine men
Angela Paine

Each plant is covered here in depth, explaining its history, myth and symbolism and also how to grow, preserve, prepare and use them. Uniquely, here, their properties are examined together with the scientific evidence that they work.

1905047622 240pp 250/153mm b/w illustrations **£16.99 $29.95**

The Healing Sourcebook
Learn to heal yourself and others
David Vennells

Here is the distilled wisdom of many years practice; a number of complementary therapies which are safe, easy to learn from a book, and combine wonderfully with each other to form a simple but powerful system of healing for body and mind.

1846940052 320pp **£14.99 $22.95**

Healing the Eternal Soul
Insights from past life and spiritual regression
Andy Tomlinson

Written with simple precision and sprinkled with ample case examples this will be an invaluable resource for those who assist others in achieving contact with the eternal part of themselves. It is an invaluable contribution and advancement to the field of Regression Therapy. More so, it is an incredibly interesting read! **Dr. Arthur E. Roffey**, Past Vice-President, Society for Spiritual Regression

190504741X 288pp **£14.99 $29.95**